Imperial Roman Naval Forces 31 BC–AD 500

Raffaele D'Amato · Illustrated by Graham Sumner

Series editor Martin Windrow

First published in Great Britain in 2009 by Osprey Publishing
Midland House, West Way, Botley, Oxford OX2 0PH, UK
443 Park Avenue South, New York, NY 10016, USA
E-mail: info@ospreypublishing.com

A CIP catalogue record for this book is available from the British Library

ISBN 978 1 84603 317 9
ebook ISBN: 978 1 84603 901 0

Editor: Martin Windrow
Page layouts by Myriam Bell Design, France
Typeset in Helvetica Neue and ITC New Baskerville
Index by Peter Finn
Originated by PPS Grasmere Ltd
Printed in China through World Print Ltd.

09 10 11 12 13   10 9 8 7 6 5 4 3 2 1

FOR A CATALOGUE OF ALL BOOKS PUBLISHED BY OSPREY MILITARY AND AVIATION PLEASE CONTACT:

Osprey Direct, c/o Random House Distribution Center,
400 Hahn Road, Westminster, MD 21157
Email: uscustomerservice@ospreypublishing.com

Osprey Direct, The Book Service Ltd, Distribution Centre,
Colchester Road, Frating Green, Colchester, Essex, CO7 7DW
E-mail: customerservice@ospreypublishing.com

Osprey Publishing is supporting the Woodland Trust, the UK's leading
Woodland conservation charity, by funding the dedication of trees.

www.ospreypublishing.com

Dedication

To my dear father Nicola and to my beloved mother Irene,
who introduced me to the glory of Rome.

Artist's note

Readers may care to note that the original paintings from which
the colour plates in this book were prepared are available for
private sale. All reproduction copyright whatsoever is retained
by the Publishers. All enquiries should be addressed to:

gs.illustrator@btinternet.com

The Publishers regret that they can enter into no correspondence
upon this matter.

Acknowledgements

A great number of people, museums, and institutions have
participated in the realization of this book. Very special thanks
must be given to Dr Annamaria Liberati, Director of the Museo
della Civiltà Romana, in Rome, first of all for her assistance in the
museum in order to take vision of the casts of Roman monuments
preserved there; and secondly for obtaining the kind permission
to publish the related photos and documentation. For the same
reason it is my duty to thank the Soprintendente Professor
Umberto Broccoli who has kindly given his permission for
the publication of such important items.
The finds of Comacchio and Voghenza, as well as other material
from Ravenna and Classe, have been published only thanks to
the precious help and collaboration of the Dr Fede Berti of the
Museo Archeologico of Ferrara, to whom I would like to express
all my gratitude for the assistance on the field. For Ravenna
material special thanks are also due to the D.ssa Maria Grazia
Maioli, of the Soprintendenza Archeologica dell'Emilia.

IMPERIAL ROMAN NAVAL FORCES 31 BC–AD 500

INTRODUCTION

Nothing is so productive of surprises as the sea....
(Tacitus, *Annals*, XIV, 3)

The glory of Imperial Rome was built by the legions that conquered most of Western Europe and the Middle East. Nevertheless, to help create and preserve this empire Rome had to establish itself as a strong naval power, able both to transport and supply her armies and to strike decisively at any potential rivals.

Incredibly, in the 3rd century BC Rome had little or no navy to speak of when she embarked on the first of three titanic struggles with the foremost seafaring power of the day, Carthage. Equally remarkably, the Romans at first copied and then surpassed the better technology of their Carthaginian enemies. The Romans' admirable capacity for organization, combined with their practical common sense, more than made up for their early deficiencies in naval equipment and tactics, and they destroyed Carthaginian maritime power forever. This victory opened the way for Rome's relentless rise, and her dominance of the Mediterranean basin for the next seven centuries.

At the close of the civil wars that brought the Republic to an end in the late 1st century BC, Caesar Octavian, soon styled Augustus, achieved imperial power after the decisive naval battle at Actium. With the advent of Empire, Rome's fleets were used to maintain internal communications and to help spread Roman civilization throughout the known world and beyond, as her sea-captains ventured as far as Scandinavia, Africa and India. Even after the disintegration of the Western Empire in the middle of the 5th century AD Rome's seapower was still strong enough to enable Justinian to reconquer Italy, North Africa and parts of Spain in the 6th century, and to dominate the Eastern Mediterranean until the rise of the Arabs in the 7th century.

Despite these remarkable achievements, the Roman navy has received scant attention by comparison with the land forces of the Empire. The author's intention in this book is to illustrate the world of Roman sailors and seaborne soldiers, by reference to ancient written and artistic sources, archaeological finds – many presented to

the general reader for the first time here – and careful reconstruction
based on this evidence. (The exact references to the ancient written
sources listed in the Bibliography are embedded in the text at the
relevant points.) While this is no place for attempting to address the
much wider subject of the tactics employed in naval warfare, a short
chapter describing the basic characteristics of various types of ships used
by the Romans is included.

CHRONOLOGY

31 BC	2 September: fleet of C.G.C. Octavianus and M.V. Agrippa, formed of light, fast *liburnae*, defeats heavier ships of M. Antonius and Cleopatra (Dio Cassius, L,18,5; Hor. *Epod.* I, 1,1), capturing 300 vessels (Plut. *Ant.* 68).
30 BC	Galatian King Aminta is charged by Octavianus to fight the Western Cilician pirates.
27–20 BC	Naval operations by Agrippa against the Cantabri in Hispania.
15 BC	Roman triremes on Lake Constance destroy fleet of the Vindelici during Raetian campaign.
12 BC	During Drusus' expedition in Germania, Roman squadron defeats rowing-boat fleet of the Bructeri on River Ems; naval operations against the Chatti aided by the Frisians.
4–5 AD	Operations by Roman North Sea fleet around Jutland peninsula.
14 AD	Germanicus' operations against Arminius include embarkation of four legions.
16 AD	Germanicus employs North Sea fleet to avoid dangerous rivers, embarking army in Rhine delta aboard *c.*1,000 ships. He attacks Germans at Amisius river estuary, using ships as military camps. Germans are defeated at the Weser, but during its return the Roman fleet is partially destroyed by storms.
28 AD	Legions in Germania transported by fleet to fortress of Flevum on the Rhine to operate against the rebellious Frisians.
47 AD	Cauci pirates led by Roman deserter Gannascus ravage Gallic coasts; Gn. Domitius Corbulo uses Rhine fleet against them. Gannascus executed, Frisian revolt suppressed.
50 AD	Formation of Roman Danube fleet.
59 AD	Involvement of Classis Praetoriae Misenatis (Misenum Fleet) personnel in Nero's murder of his mother Empress Agrippina.
67 AD	Roman naval operation in Judaea against pirates on Sea of Galilee.
68 AD	Creation of Legio I Adiutrix with marines of Classis Misenatis; following Galba's death the fleet backs Otho, carries out operations in Ligurian Gulf.

69 AD	Naval clashes during civil war between Vitellius and Vespasianus.
69–70 AD	Naval clashes on Rhine during Batavian revolt of Julius Civilis; crew of captured Roman flagship imprisoned at Augusta Trevirorum; creation of Legio II Adiutrix from marines of Classis Ravennatis (Ravenna Fleet). Legiones I and II Adiutrices and Britannica fleet operate against the rebels; minor victory of the Germanic Cannenefati against the Classis Britannica; Legio II Adiutrix awarded title 'Pia Fidelis'.
79 AD	Roman fleet based at Misenum, commanded by the historian Pliny the Elder, evacuates refugees from eruption of Mount Vesuvius; Pliny dies at Stabiae after inhaling volcanic fumes.
80 AD	Gn. Julius Agricola creates fleet for conquest of Caledonia – finally proves Britain is an island. Legio II Adiutrix stationed at Lindum (Lincoln).
90 AD	Legiones Adiutrices participate in Domitianus' Dacian campaign.
105 AD	Trajanus leaves with fleet from Brundusium (Brindisi) for his second Dacian campaign, in which Legiones Adiutrices participate; from 2nd C AD, permanent *castrum* of Legio II Adiutrix at Aquincum.
116 AD	Q. Marcius Turbo sent by Trajanus with an army and fleet against Lucuas, 'king' of the Jews.
167 AD	Increasing strategic importance of Ravenna during Marcomannic Wars.
169 AD	Legio I Adiutrix from Pannonia, under command of P. Elvius Pertinax, restores northern Italy from control of the Marcomanni and Quadi.
171 AD	Same legion recaptures Noricum and Raetia from Germanic peoples.
196–197 AD	Emperor Septimius Severus forms new naval unit, manning all the triremes in Italy with heavily armed troops for war in the East against the usurper Pescennius Niger (Herodian, II, 14,7; III, 1,1). Troops embarked on artificial canal between Tigris and Euphrates rivers: Roman army loots Parthian royal palace at Ctesiphon.
238 AD	Emperor Puppienus chooses Ravenna as base for operations against Maximinus.
238–251 AD	First Gothic War; sea and land raids by the Goths, pirate activity in Black Sea. Emperor Claudius II awards Legio II Adiutrix the title 'Constans'.
261 AD	Persian War; usurper Balista collects ships from Cilician ports and defeats Persians near Pompeiopolis, capturing harem of Sassanian King Shapur I (Zon., XII, 630; Syncellus, 7742–7743).

Terracotta lamp of c.30 BC, representing a warship in battle with an armoured crew. (British Museum)

262–266 AD	Moesia and Thracia under Gothic threat; fleet of 500 Herulian ships destroyed by Romano-Byzantine fleet off Byzantium. Barbarians ravage Greece, sacking Athens, Corinth, Argos and Sparta; Athenian leader P. Erennius Dexippus, with 2,000 men and help of Roman fleet, ambushes the barbarians on their return journey. Their army and fleet are finally destroyed by Emperor Gallienus in Thracia.
268 AD	Roman *navarcha* Probus defeats Palmyrene army before Alexandria.
269 AD	Second Gothic invasion by sea; Herulians, Borani, Goths and other Germanic peoples attack Bosphorean towns under Roman control. Some 2,000 ships and 320,000 men from the Danube enter Roman territory. M. Aurelius Claudius defeats the invaders by sea and by land; Roman fleet rebuilt.
270 AD	Borani arm Bosphorean ships, conscript captive sailors and ravage Black Sea coasts as far as Trapezunte; port falls, many Roman warships lost.
278 AD	Piracy by the Isaurian Lidius (Palfuerius) along coasts of Asia, Pamphilia and Lycia; besieged in the city of Cremna of Pisidia by Roman legions, he sacrifices men, women and children before he is killed by a traitor who allows the Romans to enter the city.
Beginning of 4th C AD	The old Legio I Adiutrix is divided into one Legio Comitatensis and one of Limitanei.

Fragments of a relief from Nola, related to the naval victory of Octavian over Antony and Cleopatra's fleet at Actium, 31 BC. (Museo della Civiltà Romana, Rome; author's photo)

323 AD	Crispus, son of Emperor Constantinus, defeats fleet of Emperor Licinius in the Dardanelles, capturing Byzantium and sinking 130 enemy ships.
Second half of 4th C AD	Pirate activity by the Isaurians in Cilicia.
400 AD	Imperial fleet of Arcadius destroys fleet of the Gothic *Magister Militum* Gainas in Sea of Marmara.
Beginning of 5th C AD	Piracy by the Mangones, slave-traders from Galatia, along the coasts of Roman North Africa. The old Legio II Adiutrix, part of which had always been stationed at Aquincum, is divided into two Legiones Comitatenses stationed in Britannia.
419 & 438 AD	Emperor Theodosius II forbids the divulging of secrets of naval carpentry, probably to avoid its spread to rising Vandal power in North Africa.
440 AD	Sea and land forces sent by Theodosius II to the West.

445–450 AD	2,000 conscripts transported on warships from Constantinople to Alexandria to put down ecclesiastical disorders.
457 AD	Western Emperor Majorianus defeats Vandal fleet commanded by relative of King Genseric, near Sinuessa in Campania.
468 AD	Joint naval expedition against Vandals by Western and Eastern fleets under General Basiliscos ends in disaster; Genseric uses fireships against Roman fleet.

THE FLEETS

In the aftermath of Actium some 800 warships were in active service, and when Octavian/Augustus took power he maintained naval strength and undertook a serious programme of reorganization.

The navy was distributed in three permanent Praetorian (or 'high seas') Fleets, stationed at Forum Iulii (modern Frejus in southern France), at Ravenna on the Adriatic coast of north-east Italy, and at Misenum near Naples in the south-west to defend the Tyrrhenian Sea. (Suet. *Div. Aug.*, XLIX). The bulk of the Antonian fleet captured at Actium was initially based at Frejus, but both the base and the fleet were soon disbanded as unnecessary. The other two fleets were maintained, their main duties being policing and convoy escort. Until the start of the 5th century the Classis Praetoria Misenatis or Misenum Fleet (bearing the title 'Pia Vindex' under Caracalla) was the main imperial naval force, thereafter losing importance to the Classis Ravennatis (Ravenna Fleet). Each of these fleets counted about 10,000 men, and the Ravenna Fleet was considerably enlarged under Vespasian.

Provincial Fleets, to defend the frontiers and support the legions in the different *provinciae*, were soon added. One of the first and strategically most important was the Rhine Fleet in Germania, whose military ports were linked by road with those in Gaul (France). At the time of Drusus' expedition in 12 BC we read that the military port of Bonna (modern Bonn), perhaps the main base of the Rhine Fleet, was directly linked with Gessoriacum (modern Boulogne – Florus 2,30). Under the early Empire the Rhine Fleet was an integral part of the army of Germania Inferior, composed of four legions in the 1st century AD, including Legio XI; this means that the soldiers of these legions could be used in the fleet as *milites classiarii* (fleet soldiers or 'marines'). During the Civilis revolt we find in the army of Germania Inferior the Legiones V and XV at Vetera, XVI and I at Novaesium (Neuss) and Bonna, serving with the Rhine Fleet. Among the additional legions sent to crush the revolt we find I Adiutrix and II Adiutrix formed from fighting sailors: later I Adiutrix was temporarily sent to Hispania, but by 88 AD we find it back in Germania Superior, then in Pannonia under Domitian. After the Civilis revolt II Adiutrix was sent to Britain, and then also to Pannonia by Domitian. A later inscription found at Baden Baden confirms the presence of this legion in Germania under Trajan.

The 1st- or 2nd-century AD funerary stele of Marcus Iulius Sabinianus, of the Praetorian Misenum Fleet, found in Athens near the church of Haghia Triada. This 'fleet soldier' or marine was recruited from the Bessi tribe of Thrace; he served for five years before dying at the age of 30. He wears at his hip a *pugio* resembling the weapon found with the remains of the famous 'Herculaneum soldier'. Note also the characteristic *paenula* cloak, the apron straps and pendants showing below the belt, the *caligae* sandals, the javelin and the round shield. The original cast of the sculpture still shows traces of red-brown colour on the tunic and *paenula*. (Cast, Museo della Civiltà Romana, Rome)

Officers of the Danube Fleet engaged in military operations against the barbarians, as seen on a sarcophagus dating from the 1st or 2nd century AD that was once preserved near the church of San Domenico in Sora. (Photo courtesy Dr Alessandra Tanzilli)

Additional fleets included the Classis Alexandrina (Alexandria) Siriaca (Syria), Moesica (patrolling the Danube), Pannonica (also on the Danube), and Britannica (improved at the time of Agricola' invasion of Scotland). A small fleet also patrolled the Euphrates.

The Classis Pontica, with 40 ships based at Trapezunte (Trabzon Turkey), was the main naval force for the defence of Asia Minor to keep under control the troublesome Pisidians, defend the north-eastern borders of the Empire and patrol the Black Se coast as far as the allied Bosphorean kingdom of Panticape (the modern Crimea). It was always necessary to keep a fleet on the alert in this region because of continuous piracy; from the time of Tiberius, Sarmatians, Scythians and later Gothic pirates ravaged the Black Sea coasts and inland towns. Whole fleets of pirates ranged the Black Sea as well as the Mediterranean. Ammianus (31,5,15) tell us that in the time of Decius the Bosphorean and Propontean coasts were ravaged by Scythian peoples (Goths) in 2,000 ships, who were even able to besiege major cities. Under Trebonianus Gallus there were further pirate incursions as far as Asia Minor and Ephesus. Two large Gothic invasions in 250–269 AD convinced the Romans of the need to maintain a powerful fleet in this vital crossroads region, and this became the basis of the permanent Imperial fleet based at Constantinople from 330 AD onwards.

In the 3rd century the coast of Britain facing the North Sea was fortified against the incursions of sea-borne raiders including Saxons, Frisians and Angles, and the Litus Saxonici (Saxon Coast command, led by a *comes*) was created. From the 4th century we also find a small fleet or squadron at Aquileia in northern Italy and on Lake Como. Squadrons patrolled the Rhone, Seine, and other major rivers in Gaul. A small fleet in the Black Sea defended the Greco-Roman inhabitants of the western and eastern shores of the Bosphorus and Asia Minor. A squadron at the extremity of the *limes* still patrolled the Rhine and was used for military operations beyond that frontier, such as the expeditions of the Emperor Julian in 361 AD, as well as for special transport missions.

ORGANIZATION

We know from Caesar that in the late Consular period warships were entrusted to tribunes and centurions, under fleet commanders or *navarcha*. The crew of a warship was usually composed of a contingent of soldiers (*milites classiarii*), armed sailors (*nautae*) – the seamen responsible for the technical duties of ship-handling but not excluded from fighting – and oarsmen (*remiges*). Traditional Greek terms are frequently employed and interchanged with the Latin terms by Roman authors to describe categories of soldiers and sailors, such as the heavily armoured *oplitai*, the *epibatai*, the *nautai* (sailors) and the *eretai* (oarsmen). Sometimes the embarked troops came from land-based legions, as occurred at Actium. Under Augustus and Tiberius the crews and commanders of ships all belonged to the *familia imperatoris*, and their military organization seems have been embryonic. It was only under Claudius that the naval forces were subjected to a more regular regime.

Officer ranks and specialists

The most senior figures in the naval hierarchy under the Empire were the commanders of the two main Italian fleets, *praefecti* of equestrian rank who were directly responsible to the emperor. Their immediate subordinates were the *subpraefecti,* sometimes of equestrian rank, with some previous military experience but not necessarily naval. The *praefecti* of the provincial fleets had lower rank than those of the Italian fleets. There also existed detached commands (*vexillationes*) comprising a part of a fleet, commanded by *praepositi* directly appointed by the fleet prefect.

According to Vegetius, the Ravenna and Misenum fleets each had one legion attached (V,1). He probably refers to the division of the 10,000 marines into cohorts for their service on land, especially in Rome, where they had permanent barracks and special duties. Each *cohors* was commanded by a 'fleet centurion'; this rank is found in inscriptions in several localities, chiefly Rome but also Civita Vecchia and Portus (Ostia) in Italy and Athens in Greece. Numerous inscriptions mentioning *centuriones classiarii* or *classici* of the Misenum Fleet are found in localities far from that fleet's base, where they commanded *vexillationes*. The leader of naval troops assigned to a land campaign was called the *praepositus vexillationis*, as in an inscription from Rome.

Stele of M. Titius Honoratus, a *classiarius* ('marine') of the Ravenna Fleet; probably from Classe, late 2nd century AD. (Museo Civico, Padua, by kind permission of the Comune di Padova, Assessorato ai Musei, Politiche Culturali e Spettacolo)

From at least the time of Nero the sources distinguish between three different ranks in the fleet: the *navarchus*, the *trierarchus* (commander of a trireme?), and the *centurio classiarius* or *classicus* (Tacitus, *Ann.*, XIV, 8 – XV, 51; Suet. *Nero*, XXIV). In inscriptions soon after that reign the term *centuria* was usually synonymous with a warship. We know from the inscription of C. Sulgius Caecilianus that in the 3rd century the rank of *centurio navarchus* was inferior to that of the legionary centurion (CIL VIII, 14854). So it seems that all the three ranks were grades of centurions, but how they were graduated, and their relationship to one another within the fleet or a single crew, remains unclear. An inscription from Baia records that the Emperor Antoninus conferred the rank of *centurio* on the *trierarchi* and *navarchi* of the Misenum Fleet, and Marcus Aurelius and Lucius Verus extended it to the *principes classis*. So, from that period, there were at least three centurion's ranks on a ship: the *trierarchus*, the *navarchus* and the *princeps*.

Naval forces and warships were entrusted to the *centuriones* who were designated as *navarchi* of *ordo tertius* (commanders of large fleets, in that case with the same ranks as the *praepositi* and *praefecti* of provincial fleets); of *ordo secundus* (small fleets or squadrons); and of *ordo primus* or *trierarchi* (trireme or *liburna* ship commanders). Lower ranks were held by *centuriones classici*, who commanded a unit of 100 *nautae,* and from the 2nd century AD corresponded in rank with their counterparts on land.

The Hadrianic-period funerary memorial of M. Herennius Valens, of the Tromentina tribe from Salona. The *cursus honorum* (career summary) records that he was an *evocatus* of Legio XI Claudia after serving as a *centurio* of that legion; a centurion in both Legiones I and II Adiutrices, then in Legio XV Apollinaris, once again in Legio I Adiutrix, then in Legio IV Flavia in the 5th Cohort of *hastati posteriores*. The relief carving shows the *vitis* or staff of centurial rank, a fringed *sagum* cloak, a heavy tunic with wide sleeves, and a large ring on the little finger of his left hand. Left of the centurion's head, and enlarged in the detail at right, is a representation of a *calo* (servant) carrying a *codex ansatus* or case for writing-tablets – a common feature on military gravestones of the 1st and 2nd centuries AD. This figure is probably the centurion's freedman (*libertus*) M. Helius Herennius, who dedicated the gravestone. (Author's photos, courtesy of Archaeological Museum, Zagreb)

Junior officers on the ships were the *optio*, the *suboptio*, the armourer (*armorum custos*), the standard-bearers (*signiferi*) and the trumpeters (*tubicines* and *cornicines*). Particular duties were performed by the *beneficiarius stolarchi* (or *stolarchus*), with rank corresponding to that of *beneficiarius* in the land forces; the *secutor trierarchi;* the *pitulus* (pitcher?); the *coementarius* (caulker), and the *subunctor* and *coronarius* – with uncertain duties, but probably related to ship maintenance. More junior levels were the *principales* or *immunes*, who performed different duties related to the equipment and the running of the ship. Among these were the helmsman (*gubernator*), his deputy or *proreta*, the *nauphylax*, the man who gave the timing to the oarsmen (*hortator*), and a musician who gave the rhythm for oar movements (*symphoniacus*). The lower ranks were the fleet soldiers/marines (*milites classiarii*), sailors (*nautae*) and *remiges* (oarsmen). The Latin jurist Ulpian says that 'in the fleet all the sailors and rowers are soldiers' (*Dig*. XXXVII, 13). So the fighting crew of a warship consisted not only of the soldiers – including the élite *propugnatores*, the *balistarii* (catapult crews) and *sagittarii* (archers) – but also all the oarsmen and other seamen.

Two *medici* (doctors) were employed on each ship, together with attendants to the sacrifices (*victimarii*), attendants to the orders, scribes and clerks. We also find mentions in sources of various other specialists. These were under the command of an *optio* and the direction of an *architectus*, the shipwright of the fleet, and were divided into *fabri navales* (carpenters), *artifices* (workers) and *velarii (*sail-makers or sail-handlers). These specialisms reflect the demanding technical nature of ship-handling; they explain why, for example, expert *classiarii* of the Misenum Fleet were employed to operate the *velarium* or canopy that protected spectators in the Coliseum from sun and rain, which was rigged in sections.

There were also a certain number of naval functionaries dealing with bureaucratic duties. Sources mention the *exceptor*, the *exactus*, the *scriba*, the *librarius* and the *rationalis*, all of them employed on active service with the fleet. By contrast, the *dispensator classis* (fleet paymaster) and the *tabularius* (file clerk) were Imperial freedmen or slaves not employed on active service.

A man's place in the *cursus honorum* (rank structure) depended not only upon his personal capabilities or military experience but also on the favour of the emperor. Centurion Aquilius, little more than an assassin hired by Septimius Severus, was appointed from the ranks to command of the *frumentarii* or spies; to *primuspilus* of Legio XI Claudia; to the command of a *vexillatio;* and finally, by way of some further institutional honours, was appointed as *Praefectus Classis Praetoriae Ravennatis*. Sometimes the quality of naval commanders was suspect. For example, at the beginning of the 5th century the defence of the North African coasts against pirates was delegated to a certain Tribune Litus, who was accused by St Augustin of taking bribes from those same Mangones pirates and slave-traders. A similar accusation was also levelled against the commander of the British Fleet, Carausius.

According to the *Notitia Dignitatum*, in the Western Empire in 430 AD the fleets of Ravenna, Aquileia, Como, Misenum, the river fleet of the Rhone and the *barcariorum* at Ebrodunum (modern Yverdon on Lake Neuchâtel) were placed under the supreme command of the *Magister Peditum* close to the Imperial Court.

Recruitment

In the early years the posting of Roman *milites* on warships was regarded as a punitive measure (*militiae mutatio*), because the soldiers did not like to fight at sea; conversely, deployment of the fighting sailors on land was regarded as a promotion. Such cross-deployments were, however, a normal military duty; *nautae* and *milites classiarii* were often engaged in land battles, and land troops were often embarked on ships. One of the 30 legions raised by Antonius, the XVII, was named 'Classica' for its service at sea.

In the early period the oarsmen (*remiges*) and sailors were usually recruited from among allied peoples (*socii navales*), or amongst the lowest class of citizens, listed by the *census*, and the *liberti* (freedmen). According to Livy, they formed the detachments of men *in classe scripti* (XXII, 57). Contrary to popular belief, service as rowers on warships was generally fulfilled by freedmen and only in exceptional circumstances by slaves. According to Dio Cassius, during the civil wars slaves were enrolled in the fleet (XLVIII, 49); however, according to Appian and Suetonius, before they were armed they were made freedmen (*Bell. Civ.*, V, 1; *Div. Aug.*, XVI). In the late Consular period Rome still relied heavily upon those non-Roman peoples who had a strong maritime tradition: Cicero, in his *Philippica* (XI,5) urged the Senate that the Proconsul C. Cassius should be

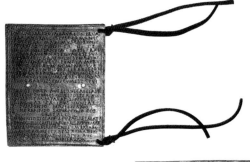

A military discharge diploma in bronze from Voghenza, dated 12 June 100 AD, and relating to the *gregalis* Lucius Bennius Beuza, a Dalmatian serving with the Ravenna Fleet. It reads, in part: 'The Emperor... Trajanus... to those who are members of the Classis Praetoria Ravennatis under the command of Lucius Cornelius Gratus and have completed 26 or more years of service, whose names are herewith listed – to them, to their sons [and] descendants, [he] has given Roman citizenship and the honour of [legally recognized] marriage with the wives they have at the moment of the concession of citizenship.... To the Gregalis Lucius Bennius Beuza, son of Licca, a Dalmatian, and his wife Moca...'. (Archaeological Museum, Ferrara; author's photo, courtesy of Dr Fede Berti)

Milites classiarii of the Danube Fleet engaged in building earthworks, 105 AD; from Trajan's Column, scene LXIV. Note the typical bunched neck-knot of the tunic. The nearest of the display of shields has a trident device at the top and bottom of the symmetrical blazon. (Cast, Museo della Civiltà Romana, Rome)

appointed to the administration of Syria and of the war against Dolabella, with the power to recruit sailors in Asia, Bithynia, Pontus and Syria. One reason given for the defeat of Antony at Actium was that his crews were 'made up of all sorts of races', and that they were not reliable because 'as they had been wintering at a distance from him, they had had no practice and their numbers had been diminished by disease and desertions'. The fleets of vassal kings were often used to prevent piracy, like that of the Bosphorean King Sauromates who, at time of Augustus, operated with his own fleet against the Tauri and other pirates in the Black Sea.

At the end of the Republic recruitment amongst allies was soon the only source for the *classiarii* and *nautae,* because the formerly unemployed slaves, *liberti* and *proletarii* who had been the potential recruits now had numerous employment opportunities during the reconstruction of the Roman state after the chaos of the civil wars. For a while the *classiarii* consequently did not enjoy the same level of prestige as the land forces; a veteran of Antony's army before the battle of Actium was quoted thus: '…an infantry centurion, a man who had fought many a battle for Antony and was covered with scars, burst into laments as Antony was passing by, and said, "General, why dost thou distrust these wounds and this sword and put thy hopes in miserable logs of wood? Let Egyptians and Phoenicians do their fighting at sea, but give us land, on which we are accustomed to stand and either conquer our enemies or die"'.

In the early Empire it was seen as raising the status of the naval soldiers when emperors incorporated them into the legions, or created 'additional' legions from amongst their numbers; such legions were uniquely distinguished by the title *adiutrices.* Conversely, it was a punishment for mutinous soldiers to be incorporated into the naval forces. According to Suetonius, Nero made regular soldiers (*classiarii* or *iuxti milites*) from rowers and marines of the Misenum Fleet, enlisting them in a regular infantry corps (*Galba*, XII). When Galba wanted to return them to their former duties they refused, and demanded back the eagle and standards, so they were slaughtered after a cavalry charge at the Milvian Bridge and the survivors decimated. However, there were still enough left for Galba to form the nucleus of Legio I Adiutrix. When Otho took power after the assassination of Galba he decided to invade Narbonese Gaul by sea, and his fleet, according to Tacitus, was 'a strong and reliable army, devoted to the cause' (*Hist.*, I, 87). He granted to all marines hopes of honourable service, and strengthened the legion with some of the survivors of the Milvian Bridge massacre who had been imprisoned by Galba. By contrast, Legio II

Adiutrix was formed from amongst the elite of the marines of the Ravenna Fleet, whose crews were composed of Dalmatians; these passed in turn from Vitellius' to Vespasian's service, and demanded permission to serve in his legions (Tac., *Hist.*, III, 50).

Over time, service in the naval arm grew in status. Local Italians were even recruited as sailors for provincial ships, although the crews were multinational and usually foreigners were preferred. During a naval clash on the Rhine during the Civilis rebellion of 69 AD the rebels attacked a squadron of the Rhine Fleet, and the crews, mainly composed of Batavi and a Tungrian cohort, joined the revolt and killed their Italic former comrades.

That the main recruitment was amongst provincials rather than citizens (*peregrini*) is proved by numerous finds of military diplomas giving these men Roman citizenship upon their discharge. On gravestones their non-Roman origin is proved by the absence of the *praenomen* of the father, which was usual in the case of citizens. Epigraphic documents also show that for the most part the *classiarii* were recruited in provinces where there was a long seafaring tradition, mainly in the Greek-speaking provinces such as Egypt, Asia Minor, Paphlagonia, Thrace and especially Syria. In Egypt the recruitment of Greek citizens into the auxiliary militia was the rule, while a great number of native Egyptians were incorporated into the fleet, especially in later centuries. The Latin-speaking countries favoured for *classiarii* recruitment were Sardinia, Corsica, Pannonia, and especially Illyria-Dalmatia. Dio of Prusa in Bithinia remembers how, in the 2nd century AD, the Rhodians were obliged to provide the Roman fleet at Corinth with one or two small ships (*Orationes*, 31, 620), but he commented that since their previous obligations had been much greater they should be happy that their duties had been much reduced.

Miles of a Legio Adiutrix, from a monument of the time of Marcus Aurelius, second half of 2nd century AD. The shield blazon is similar to one seen on the Praeneste relief of almost 200 years earlier. (*in situ*, Constantine Arch, Rome; author's collection)

Terms of service

The terms of service varied over time. Most military diplomas attest a length of service of 26 years, which was raised to 28 under the 3rd-century emperors Philippus and Trajan Decius – after 26 years' service the *miles* was called a *veteranus* and received double pay (*duplarius*). A splendid specimen of military diploma to the *gregalis* Lucius Bennius Beuza, of Dalmatian origin, has recently been found in Vicus Habentia (modern Voghenza, Italy). Such documents, comparable to a modern notarized certificate attested by witnesses, were engraved on two bronze tablets linked like a booklet. The diploma conferred upon the recipient and his sons Roman citizenship, and recognized the veteran's *connubium* (marriage, i.e. usually an acknowledgement of a union which already existed). Before 213 AD, when Caracalla conferred Roman citizenship on all free-born people living within the borders of the Empire, it was presented – for a fee – to auxiliary cavalrymen, infantrymen and marines at the time of their discharge. The text was impressed in duplicate: one copy engraved in small letters on the external surface so that it was possible to read it at a glance, the second on the inside surface together with the names of the witnesses, which confirmed its legitimacy. A further copy was retained in the Tabularium in Rome itself. Like *veterani* of the land forces, naval veterans could also be recalled to service at need, as happened to C. Nonius Calvisius of the Misenum Fleet, who received the title of *veteranus evocatus*.

In the Imperial period, while serving in the fleets, marines had all the same legal rights as land troops. *Navarchi* and *trierarchi* were allowed to draw up their wills following the military law (*de iure militari*). Each soldier received the usual basic pay, as attested on the gravestone of L. Didius Ruber, *miles simplarius* serving in the Ravenna Fleet aboard the trireme 'Neptunus'. Their pay was augmented in the case of prolonged service. There are also attested marines with the qualification of *duplicarii* or *duplarii*, and also a *librarius sesquiplaris* from the time of Decius (CIL III LVI); this corresponds to the distinction made by Vegetius between *simplares*, *duplares* and *sesquiplares* in the land army, meaning soldiers receiving twice or even six times the basic pay rate (II, 7).

The state supplied food and clothing. Their rations comprised a special bread very similar to the modern ship's biscuit, and strong wine. Like the usual military bread the sailors' ration was probably made with coarse flour (Pliny the Elder, *Hist. Nat.* XXII, 68). Plautus informs us that the sailors made heavy use of garlic and leeks in their diet (*Poenulus*, V, 5). Pliny the Elder also said that they drank a very poor wine – as a sign of his soldierly hardiness Cato boasted that he could drink even that (*Hist. Nat.* XIV, 23).

Duties ashore

Apart from their service with the fleets sailors and marines were employed for a range of civil duties. From the time of Claudius two cohorts were permanently established in Puteoli (modern Pozzuoli) and Ostia, to guard against the danger of fires (Suet., *Claud.*, 25). As already mentioned, sailors operated the great *velarium* of the Coliseum, by means of pulleys (*trochlea*) and ropes passing through one or more blocks. In the time of Commodus they were still employed in this capacity, perhaps even in the Circus Maximus as well, since on one occasion that emperor ordered them to slay spectators whom he believed were laughing at him (SHA, *Comm.*, 15). *Classiarii* also appear in a list of soldiers moving the scenery at another venue in 212 AD. These *classiarii* were garrisoned in Rome specifically for these performances, and therefore had their own *castra* (camp) within the city. That of personnel from the Misenum Fleet was located in the 3rd region (Isis and Moneta), that of the Ravenna men on the other side of the Tiber. These *classiarii* were also entrusted with the transportation of weapons through the city, often by means of boats (Suet., *Otho*, VIII).

When on campaign on land the *classiarii* participated together with the land troops in the construction of earthworks, as clearly stated by Pseudo-Hyginus in his work 'On the fortifications of military camps' (*De Munitionis Castrorum*). This author, writing at the time of Trajan, says that the *classici* (naval troops) were positioned at the head of the column because it was their duty to go out first, to open and clear the way for the rest of the army, in effect acting like the pioneers of later armies (24): 'The *alae miliariae* and the *quingenariae* are stretching out, as well as the

Equites Mauri, the *Pannonii Veredarii* and all the naval troops, who first go out to clear the ways... while working, they are protected by the *Equites Mauri* and the *Pannonii Veredarii'.* This description finds a perfect match on Trajan's Column, where the sailors are represented beside their shields clearing the Dacian forest for the passage of the troops.

Many sources record the employment of *classiarii* in building work. Sailors of the African Fleet took part at the construction of the large aqueduct of Saldae in modern Tunisia, while the British Fleet sent a detachment to help in the construction of Hadrian's Wall. An inscription from Salona mentions the sailors of the trireme 'Concordia', of the Ravenna Fleet, participating in the building of the city's walls. A *vexillatio* of the Germanic Fleet at Brohl was also employed to work in local quarries, under the command of a *trierarchus* fulfilling the functions of a centurion.

One of the most intriguing discoveries related to the naval forces was made in 1982 during excavation of the ancient harbour at Herculaneum. A skeleton was found sprawled face down on the pumice-covered sand; it was the body of a man caught by the sudden eruption of Vesuvius on 25 August 79 AD, and been buried under 8in of ash. His misfortune was a golden opportunity for archaeology, because he was armed with a sword and dagger on military belts, and had a bag of carpenter's tools that survived relatively intact. These were on his shoulders, enclosed in a leather bag that appeared to have been slung over the man's back. Together with the weapons they were helpful in identifying him as a *faber navalis* of the only possible fleet in this region, the Classis Misenatis. He also had, worn in the *ventralis* of his belt, gold and silver coins of the Emperor Nero. The skeleton revealed three missing front teeth, probably

During the Severan period, at the turn of the 2nd/3rd centuries AD, Marcus Annius Severus from Philippopolis was an ex-centurion and a *veteranus* of the Misenum Fleet. We read that a certain Severus, *miles classiarium,* accused the future Emperor Didius Julianus of plotting against Commodus; perhaps he is our man, and he was promoted centurion as a reward? The stele shows a short-sleeved, belted, knee-length tunic worn with a short *paenula,* a *gladius* slung on his left hip, *caligae,* and the usual centurion's *vitis.* (Courtesy Prof I. Topalilov)

lost in a fight, while an abnormal lump in the femur of his left leg was possibly the result of a healed stabbing wound; nevertheless the rounded shaft of the femur was a sign of good nutrition and all-round healthy muscular constitution. His adductor tubercle was slightly enlarged, probably because, as a marine soldier-carpenter, he usually held heavy timbers between his knees.

CLOTHING

Cloaks and tunics

The general impression is that fighting sailors (*nautae*) and embarked troops were slightly better dressed than normal infantry, even with clothing reinforced to help resist wear and salt water. Cassius Dio specifically speaks about the use of *pachea imatia*, i.e. heavy cloaks (L, XXXIV, 5). Clothing obviously varied with climate: for instance, crews of the *nautae Parisiaci* are shown with heavy cloaks of the *paenula* or *lacerna* type, while the sailors of the Danube Fleet represented upon Trajan's Column (scene LXIX) are clad in the typical short-sleeved or sleeveless tunic with the bunched, knotted neck. This tunic was worn like a Greek *exomis*, leaving the right shoulder uncovered, and was a practical garment for manual workers, soldiers, sailors and fishermen.[1]

Gravestones from Athens show marines in the short sleeveless tunic and *sagum* cloak. Statius Rufinus, whose tombstone was found in the Keramikos cemetery in Athens, was probably of Greek origin, and served as a *classiarius* of the Misenum Fleet in the mid-2nd century AD; his *sagum* has a small tassel visible on the lower left corner. In a papyrus letter from Karanis, dating from the first half of the 2nd century AD, the *classiarius* Claudius Terentianus serving with the Alexandria Fleet thanks his father for a *paenula*, a *tunica* and *fasciae* for the legs, and also asks him to send a *byrrus castalinus*, which was a short, perhaps hooded cloak (Michigan VIII 467, inventory Code 5391 – Michigan APIS record 2445). Although the meaning of the adjective *castalinus* is unclear it might be an alternative spelling of *castorinus* – therefore a *byrrus* made of beaverskin, which would be perfectly plausible for a garment worn at sea. Moreover, he asks for a *tunica bracilis* (i.e. with sleeves) and *bracae* (short trousers), which corresponds with images on 2nd-century tombstones, and with others on Trajan's Column showing the *classiarii* wearing short trousers or *feminalia* as used by the other *milites* and *auxilia*.

Like those of ordinary soldiers, the *paenulae* cloaks of marines came in shorter and longer versions. That represented on the Severan-period *stela* (gravestone) of the former Centurion M. Annius Severus, from Philippopolis, is very short, reaching only to the waist; that of the Centurion C. Aemilius Severus is also very short, and decorated with two vertical stripes or *clavi*, originally in a contrasting colour. A fragment of illustrated papyrus roll (Paris, Bibl. Nat. Suppl. Gr. 1294), variously dated between the 2nd and 4th centuries AD, represents a soldier in the East – probably a marine from Egypt or Syria – quarrelling with a woman over a large amount of money;

Part of a leather garment, probably a military jerkin (*subarmale*), from the Comacchio ship, last quarter of the 1st century BC. It shows signs of stitched-on repair patches and/or reinforcement. (From original excavation drawings; Archaeological Museum, Ferrara, courtesy Dr Fede Berti)

---

1 For detailed information on types of Roman garment, see MAA 374, *Roman Military Clothing (1) 100 BC–AD 200*; MAA 390, *(2) AD 200–400*; and MAA 425, *(3) AD 400–640*.

he is dressed in a blue *paenula* decorated with the same two vertical bands as seen on the Severus monument, of a dark purple colour. A longer version of the *paenula*, rolled up as a *sagum* and worn with a small *tunica*, is visible on a monument of the late 2nd century related to T. Honoratus, a *classiarius* of the Ravenna Fleet.

A thick tunic, with a heavy *sagum* and short trousers, seems to be the standard dress of the 3rd century naval soldier, and is well represented on the stele of T. Flavius Sabestianus. This heavy, perhaps protective type of clothing is similar to that worn by many other Roman soldiers of this date and represented on figurative monuments, such as the Dura Europos frescoes. The use of fringed cloaks of *lacerna* type by naval personnel is attested by its wear by a commander of a dockyard or *fabrica navalis*, represented on a gilt glass vessel-cover of Tetrarchic or Constantinian period. His *lacerna*, fastened on the right side by a round *fibula* of blue colour, is worn over the usual *tunica militaris* of late 3rd–4th century type decorated with round *orbiculi, clavi* and a couple of bands (*loroi* or *segmenta*) at the wrists. Some marines are depicted on their tombstones wearing around the waist a simple cloth belt (*zona militaris*) with fringes, to which the sword appears to be fastened.

Footwear

The use of *caligae* (sandals) as military shoes is widely attested by both stelae and archaeological finds from the first three centuries. The most ancient specimens come from the Comacchio (Valle Ponti) ship. They were strong, fastened high on the ankle, low-cut, only sometimes furnished with nails, and dressed internally with a small sock or a slipper of soft leather. Shoes were often worn together with woollen socks, a detail confirmed by the tombstone of Statius Rufinus and by the above-mentioned Egyptian papyrus. In another letter to his father Terentianus mentions a pair of low-cut leather boots (*caligae*) and a pair of *udones* or felt stockings. (After reading the correspondence of Terentianus, one is tempted to ask what the state actually did supply to its marines...). *Caligae* are shown on the feet of the *optio* Montanus in the second half of the 1st century AD, and are still worn by Annius Severus some 150 years later.

Other footwear visible on the stelae are short, closed *calcei* boots; that of Rufinus shows them worn together with short *braccae* (trousers). The use of *calcei* is further confirmed by the request addressed to the Emperor Vespasian by the sailors from the Misenum Fleet detached to work on the Coliseum canopy, to pay them higher *calciarium* or 'boot money' because of the frequent wear of their shoes on the march from Naples to Rome. (In reply the thrifty emperor ordered them to march barefoot – Suet., *Div. Vesp.*, VIII). On the day of his death Pliny the Elder, commander of the Misenum Fleet, was wearing simple boots called *soleae* (Pliny the Younger, Ep. VI, 16, 5).

Headgear

Various kinds of hats and caps were typically used by naval personnel. The *pilos*, a conical felt hat used since the Etruscan Age, is often represented in figurative monuments related to sailors. It was still worn in the 3rd and 4th centuries: in a famous 3rd century mosaic representing Odysseus and the Sirens the captain of the ship is represented with a white *pilos* and white *exomis*. The *petasus* or *scutula*, of Greek origin, was a wide cap worn by travellers and sailors: a magnificent specimen in leather was recovered from Vindonissa. Sometimes in the shape of the similar ancient Greek *causia*, this was still typical of marines in the late 3rd century AD, at least in Britannia. It is not only visible on a coin of Carausius but also on the reverse of the gold medallion of Constantius Chlorus depicting his triumphal entry into London in 296 AD; the emperor is wearing it, and so are the soldiers of his victorious fleet, represented on the medallion by a single ship. The crew represented on the 5th-century *Vergilius Romanus* codex are wearing thick felt Phrygian caps (*kamelaukia*), which are still mentioned for fighting sailors in the 10th-century book *De Ceremoniis* of Constantinus Porphyrogenitus.

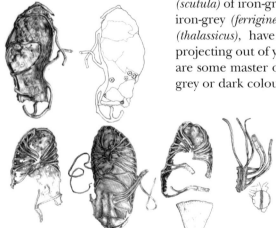

Specimens of *caligae* from the Comacchio ship, last quarter of the 1st century BC. (From original excavation drawings; Archaeological Museum, Ferrara, courtesy Dr Fede Berti)

Colours

Specific clothing colours identified *nautae, classiarii* and naval commanders. In the Consular period, Plautus (*Mil. Glor.*, IV, 4, 43, 1178ff), writing about the ordinary sailors, mentions tunics in an iron-grey colour in a description of the *nauta*'s dress: 'Take care to come here dressed in the garb of a master of a ship. Have on a broad-brimmed hat (*scutula*) of iron-grey, a woollen shade (*lanea*) before your eyes; have on an iron-grey (*ferrigineum*) cloak (*palliolum*) – for that is the seaman's colour (*thalassicus*), have it fastened over the left shoulder, your right arm projecting out of your clothes some way well girded up – pretend that you are some master of a ship.' Sailors retained their preference for an iron-grey or dark colour in the Imperial period.

Blue seems to have been the favourite colour for naval soldiers, at least for the senior ranks. Sky-blue was also associated with the navy because it was linked with Neptune, god of the oceans, and Cassius Dio says a cerulean-blue cloak or costume was the prerogative of the victorious admiral (*stolé kuanosis*, XLVIII, 48): in 43 BC Sextus Pompeius received from the Senate the title of *Praefectus Classis et Orae Marittimae* (Admiral of the Fleet and Roman Shores), and wore a mid-blue cloak, according to both Appianus (*Hist.*, V, 100) and Cassius Dio. This '*venetus*' was the colour sacred to Neptune. After his naval victory over Octavian off the coast of Sicily, Sextus Pompeius 'believing himself in very truth to be the son of Neptune… put on a dark blue robe…'. The same colours are mentioned for Agrippa's clothing, and appear, for example, in the Palestrina mosaic, if the identification by Fuentes is correct. Fuentes also suggests that the scarf (*focale*) was used as a means of identification; if so, it is possible that marines wore blue scarves and that legions raised from among the marines may have retained them.

Although various shades of blue were the most widely used they were not the only colours. Traces of red are in fact still visible on funerary monuments of marines of the Misenum Fleet, which show the red-brown colour of Praetorian soldiers who were probably employed for the units of Italic origin which also served at sea. On the gravestone of Julius Sabinianus, a *classiarius* of a vexillation of the Misenum Fleet based at Athens, traces of red were once visible on both his tunic and cloak.

White seems to have been a prerogative of the Eastern Fleet. Suetonius mentions an episode in which '…it happened that from an Alexandrian ship which had just arrived there the passengers and sailors *(nautae),* clad in pure white *(candidus),* crowned with garlands, and burning incense, lavished upon [Augustus] good wishes and the highest praise, saying that it was through him that they… sailed the seas'. White is the most visible colour for tunics in the Fayoum portraits of the 1st–2nd centuries AD; many of the soldiers portrayed could be members of the Alexandria Fleet, a theory further supported by the fact that many of these individuals wear blue cloaks. The above-mentioned 3rd-century mosaic of Odysseus, in the Bardo Museum (Tunisia), shows armed sailors or marines clad in white tunics with red *clavi* and in blue-green (*venetus*) cloaks. This mosaic could have been inspired by some of the marines operating on the North African coast (See Plate H).

In the late Empire the sailors and the troops embarked on the *naves exploratoriae* or *pictae* (i.e. the painted ships for exploratory duties) wore tunics of a blue-green colour (*venetus*), at least during the lifetime of Vegetius (IV, 37). This colour was, according to Corippus, the same as that of the blue faction at the Circus (*veneta*). The reason why sailors and marine troops wore such a *veneta vestis* was that this colour was *marinis fluctibus similis*, 'similar to the sea waves'. Vegetius states that this colour was used not only for tunics but also for the sails of the ships, so as to escape detection more easily by day and night.

The *Vergilius Romanus* codex – dated to the last quarter of the 5th century and originating in Italy, Gaul or Britain – shows Roman marines wearing heavy cloaks in red and orange pinned by crossbow *fibulae*, and tunics with *segmenta* of orange and green.

Funerary stele of Titus Flavius Sabestianus, a marine of the Misenum Fleet from Rodosto, Bulgaria, 244–249 AD, whose inscription identifies him as serving on the trireme 'Victoria'. He wears a notably thick cloak and tunic, probably of heavy wool and felt, over calf-length trousers – see Plate E2. (Courtesy of Archaeological Museum, Istanbul)

Distinctions

Like their counterparts on land, centurions of the fleet had as their main symbol of authority the *viti* or vine-staff. Gravestones shows different sizes: a shorter, with a ball-like end, e.g. on the monument of M. Annius Severus, and a longer and typically twisted type, such as that carried by C. Aemilius Severus. A staff or *virga* is also held by the above-mentioned commander of a *fabrica navalis* of the Tetrarchic or Constantinian period; this has the same mushroom-shaped top as other 3rd- or 4th-century officers' staffs. On many other military monuments of that period a mushroom-topped staff is also associated with a fringed cloak of *lacerna* type, and they might therefore be indicative of the same rank. The *Digestus* (I, 6–7) mentions a *optio fabricae* charged to oversee the soldiers working in the dockyard (*fabricenses*, CIL VII 49); so perhaps the officer shown on the gilt glass find was an *optio fabricae navalis*.

The main military decoration for admirals who won great naval victories was the *corona rostrata*, a golden crown ornamented with the prows of ships (*rostra*), visible in combination with the castellated *corona muralis* on the head of M. Vipsanius Agrippa in coins of 18 BC. Dio Cassius claims that this (double?) award was 'never attributed to anyone else, either before or after' (XLIX, 14). Among the other military decorations, the sources mention the *corona navalis* awarded to the victorious Imperator who achieved success against an enemy fleet or, allegorically, against the Ocean (Suet., *Div. Claud.*, XVII), and M.V. Agrippa is also shown on many coins with this simpler naval crown. Ordinary soldiers who were victors in sea-battles were given a simpler crown of olive-leaves.

ARMOUR AND WEAPONS

EARLY EMPIRE

Helmets

The general impression given by the monuments and sources related to the *classici milites* (CIL, V, 938) and the fighting sailors is that of light troops with a wide variety of weapons; Cassius Dio says that Octavian's marines were good swimmers and had light equipment (XLIX, 3,5). However, although their weaponry was in general lighter than that of infantry and cavalry, many sea-going soldiers did wear heavy equipment (*idem*, XLIX, 6,4, on the difference between unarmoured marines and embarked *oplitai*).

Artistic sources of the 1st century BC provide evidence for the use of helmets of Montefortino and Buggenum type, and even Late Hellenistic types complete with cheek-guards. The Praeneste ship relief today preserved in the Vatican Museum comes from the funerary monument of an Antonian *navarcha*, and is one of the best-known sources for the maritime equipment of the late Consular period. The soldiers represented wear helmets of Attic shape and Greek typology, sometimes furnished with metallic crests, while other *classiarii* are wearing the Etrusco-Corinthian helmet used by the Romans since the Age of Kings. However, only some of the helmets are pertinent to the original sculpture, although the heads restored in the 19th century imitated the originals. One original, still in place, shows the use of side-feathers on a helmet of Etrusco-Corinthian type.

The *nautae Parisiaci* represented in the famous pilaster of Tiberian date from the Ile de la Cité in Paris are wearing simple helmets of probable Coolus-Mannheim type, or even felt caps.

One of the soldiers of the Legio Adiutrix represented on the Mainz column base is wearing an incised helmet of Imperial Gallic pattern (so-called 'Weisenau' type) with a dolphin engraved on it; this is a clear naval symbol, as is the shell fibula that fastens the cloak of the *signifer* represented on the other pilaster of the same monument. Marine soldiers thus retained images and symbols of the power of Neptune on their equipment. The *classiarii* officers fighting against the barbarians on the Danube, on a sarcophagus variously dated between the 1st and 2nd centuries AD, have helmets of old Italic types complete with *geminae pinnae* and a rigid horsehair crest.

Body armour

Different types are illustrated on the Praeneste relief. A warrior with an Etrusco-Corinthian helmet wears a muscled cuirass in metal or molded leather with a simple row of linen lappets (*pteryges*), as does a second man on the prow of the ship. The use of lighter leather armour would be practical for the mobility required for fighting on board ship, and for anyone unfortunate enough to fall overboard. Nevertheless, their equipment was no less functional than that of the ordinary infantry *milites*: Cassius Dio wrote that Octavian's men at Actium were well protected by their armour against enemy blows (L, 32). The senior officer on the second row of the Praeneste relief – perhaps a Fleet Prefect, and probably the man for whom the monument was raised – wears a splendid Hellenic *thorax lepidotos* or scale armour, furnished with shoulder-pieces and a double skirt of fringed *pteryges*. Knotted on his breast by the so-called 'knot of Hercules' is the *zona militaris*, the cloth sash widely employed by Hellenic officers.

A rare find from a Roman ship confirms the use of metal muscled armour. This exceptional bronze piece was recovered near Cueva del Jarro, Spain, from a Roman shipwreck with associated amphorae of types used in the late 1st to early 3rd centuries AD; it may have belonged to a senior ship's officer, or equally to a marine armed like those on the Praeneste relief. The funerary stele of the Optio Montanus from Classe shows a muscle cuirass with hanging *pteryges* at the shoulders and a skirt of fringed strips. This can be interpreted as a representation of a *subarmale* (under-armour garment), presumably made of felt and linen, that the sculptor

Muscled bronze *lorica*, 1st–3rd century AD, from a Roman shipwreck off Cueva del Jarro, Almuñécar, Spain. Height approximately 40cm (15.75in). (Author's photo, courtesy Museo Arqueologico y Etnologico, Granada)

OPPOSITE **Details of a helmet, marines and a helmsman, from a funerary monument of the 1st century BC–1st century AD in the Cimitero dei Giordani, Rome. This remarkable monument shows marines in action on a *liburna*, armed with shields and spears. The helmet detail (top) corresponds to specimens of the Late Hellenistic period. Note the helmsman (third image down) who seems be equipped with muscled armour, probably in view of his vulnerably exposed position. Note (bottom image) the castellated bulwark, and the longitudinal row of overlapping oval *scuta* to protect the oarsmen. (Cast, Museo della Civiltà Romana, Rome)**

Details of the armour and shields of the crew of the bireme on the Praeneste monument, c.30 BC. This is our best image of marines and fighting sailors – *milites classiarii* and *propugnatores* – of the period of the battle of Actium. (Musei Vatican, Rome)

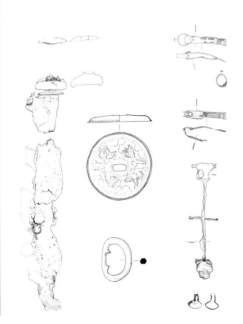

Sword from the Comacchio ship, last quarter of 1st century BC. (From original excavation drawings; Archaeological Museum, Ferrara, courtesy Dr Fede Berti)

took great care to represent as both thick and padded. The *classiarii* officers on the above-mentioned Danube battle sarcophagus wear muscled breastplates of either metal or leather.

Beside cuirasses made of leather (*corium*) and metal, monuments of late Consular and early Imperial date represent marines protected by armours made of heavy strips of padded material, probably felt (*coactile*). Corselets of felt (*coactilia*) or pressed linen, forming armours shaped in Egyptian style, are represented upon a terracotta relief preserved in the British Museum, associated with the battle of Actium. The use of padded material (*neurikà*) as body protection is still attested in the medieval sources for the naval fighters of Byzantium.

The advancing legionary on the Mainz column base is protected only by a heavy tunic superimposed over another furnished with short sleeves. The use of both leather and metallic versions of the *lorica segmentata* in the 1st–2nd centuries AD is remembered by a old relief from Madrid once in the collection of the Duke of Medina; although probably heavily restored in modern times, it represents a naval battle, where *milites classiarii* clad in such *loricae* and protected by rectangular shields are throwing missiles and shooting arrows. Their armour is worn over a *subarmale* furnished with lappets (*cymation*) and hanging *pteryges*. Three of the represented armoured warriors are clad in muscle armour, probably of leather.

On Trajan's Column the equipment of two *classiarii* depicted transferring supplies to a small river boat is very light; they are clad in leather and short mail corselets with scalloped edges, and their *gladii* are hanging on the right side of the body like those the regular legionaries.

Shields

Sources of the 1st century BC attest to the use of rectangular and oval *scuta* by *classiarii* wearing only short tunics. The old 'barleycorn' shield of Fayoum type was still employed by marines of the late 1st century BC, as depicted in the British

Museum terracotta relief. The shields of the marines represented on the Praeneste bireme are oval *scuta,* and are an important source for representations of the *episemata* (blazons) of naval soldiers. Some of them have engraved motifs, the most striking depicting a hand holding Neptune's trident and the wings of an eagle. There is a double grip system corresponding with the upper arm and the shield's boss. These blazons might relate to those of the Antonian legions; others, representing vegetal spirals and wings, show similarities with shields engraved upon monuments from Narbonne in France, which are probably devices of Caesar's Legio II Alaudae and Legio XI fighting for Octavian. The shield with Neptune's trident is certainly the device of a legion of *classiarii,* because the same device is visible on monuments of the Imperial period representing marines or soldiers from the *legiones adiutrices.* The figures of *nautae Parisiaci* of Tiberian date also have oval and rectangular shields of Celtic type fitted with circular bosses; their spears and heavy folded tunics are similar to those on the Mainz monument.

The legionaries on the Mainz column base, probably men of Legio I Adiutrix, have rectangular convex shields typical of the late 1st century AD; their blazon, formed by what seems to be a metallic application, is the stylised winged eagle of Jupiter. The shields of the *classiarii* engaged in road-building in scene LXVIII of Trajan's Column are of hexagonal shape, decorated with vegetal and floral patterns ending in a trident. Other iconographic sources show blazons for marine legions; for Legio II Adiutrix a votive altar from Pannonia Superior records the winged horse Pegasus.

Most interesting is the depiction on some stelae of what might be leather shields. Medieval sources describing Eastern Roman military equipment state that in the 10th century leather shields called *dorkai* (from which the *targa* of the later Middle Ages) were used by Imperial naval élite troops from Pamphylia. This might suggest that the use of leather shields by naval personnel could have originated in the classical Roman age (e.g. that depicted on the tombstone of Sabinianus from Athens).

Weapons

A *hasta navalis* is mentioned among the various types of spear in use in the late Consular period. Its shape is perhaps visible on an interesting relief dated to the first half of the 1st century BC showing Roman marines equipped with shields furnished with a boss and raised spine, Montefortino helmets, and a spear with a wide triangular blade, since the same blade is also visible on the Praeneste monument. *Pila* are also mentioned in sources of the early Empire (Prop., IV, 6,22) as being used in naval clashes. The equipment of the sailors in the Paris monument is very similar to that of the Celtic auxiliaries of late Republican/early Augustan period, and spears and swords loaded on a ship are visible on a stone fragment representing a ship on the Seine.

The senior officer on the Praeneste relief is the only one armed with a sword, worn on a baldric crossing his right shoulder. Similar details can be seen on a coin of 46–45 BC representing Gn. Pompeius on the deck of a warship. When Tacitus describes the murder of Agrippina by a centurion and a *trierarchus* of marines, Centurion Obaritus is armed with a *pugio* or *gladius* while Trierarch Herculeius carries a cudgel (*fustis*). A good scabbarded specimen of sword was found on the Herculaneum marine's

Full-length *gladius* of Pompei type and scabbard detail, found on the body of a *faber navalis*, 79 AD, Herculaneum. (Photos Foglia, Naples; Soprintendenza Speciale ai Beni Archeologici di Napoli e Pompei)

Military *pugio* found on the same body from Herculaneum. (Photo Foglia, Naples; Soprintendenza Speciale ai Beni Archeologici di Napoli e Pompei)

body; this single-edged weapon of Pompeian type was placed on the right side of the body, and a *pugio* was still attached to a second plated *cingulum*. The quality of the gear shows that marines of the Italian fleets might be equipped with costly items and that these were not solely reserved to the officer class. The silver-plate belt and sword scabbard fittings, including a chape with palmate details, were probably produced by local smiths around Misenum. On the Montanus *cippus* a sword is also visible; a curiosity of this image is the long decorated baldric over the right shoulder, probably not meant to support a weapon but perhaps some form of military decoration. One of the officers of the Danube Fleet represented on the 2nd-century AD sarcophagus is armed with a long knife (*culter*) having a slightly curved blade.

The axe (*dolabra*) was apparently one of the favourite weapons of marines from very early times. It was used when the *dolatores* cut the ropes and sails of enemy ships and also those of grapnels thrown aboard their own vessels. According to Cassius Dio, sailors at Actium were armed with axes (*axinai* L, 33,7). In the above-mentioned letter from Karanis, Terentianus asks his father for a battle sword (*gladius pugnatorius*), an axe (*dolabra*), a grapnel (*copula*) and two spears (*longae*). His father evidently supplied him with good-quality equipment; in the next surviving letter Terentianus asks for a new *dolabra*, because the first one had been appropriated by his *optio*!

Other obvious weapons for fighting at sea were bows and slings. Antony embarked a large number of archers (*toxotai*) and slingers (*sphendonitai*), together with heavily armed *oplitai* (Dio Cassius, L, 18, 23, 33); 'he had built lofty towers, and he had put aboard a large number of men, who could thus fight from walls'. Octavian preferred especially heavily armoured infantry (*tetragmenoi*, L, 31,3; 32,2). During the battle of Actium the Antonians bombarded the approaching ships with dense showers of stones and arrows, and cast-iron grapnels ('iron hands'). Long pikes (*kontoi*) were also used in the fighting between sailors and marines (L, 34, 7).

Silver fittings from *cingula* weapons belts also found on the body from Herculaneum, now in Museo Archeologico Nazionale, Naples. Both ends of the belt plates were rolled over to form a tube for a spindle with bulbous terminals, passing through pseudo-hinges. (Photos G. D'Auria; Soprintendenza Speciale ai Beni Archeologici di Napoli e Pompei)

Relief with naval *tubicen* and *cornicen*, from Ostia, 1st century AD. (Photos courtesy Dr Stefano Izzo)

(continued on page 33)

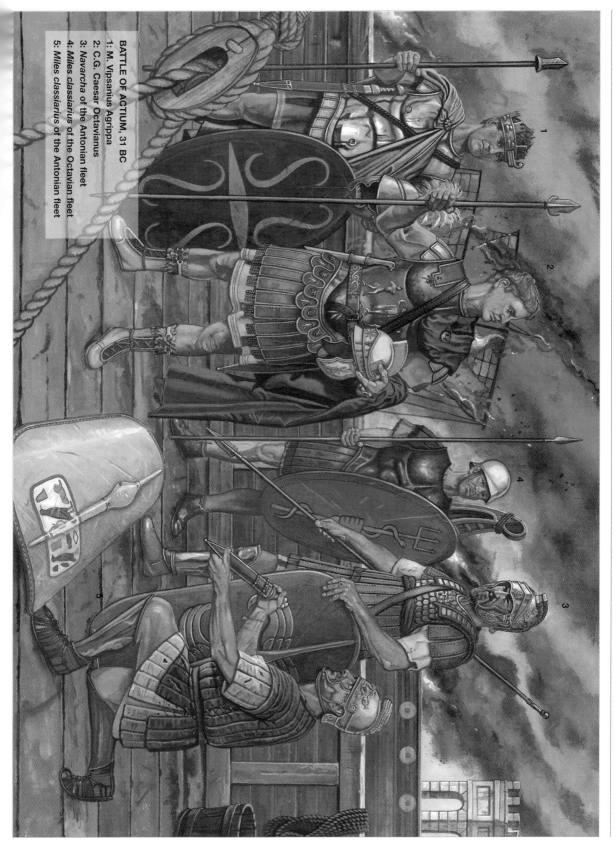

BATTLE OF ACTIUM, 31 BC
1: M. Vipsanius Agrippa
2: C.G. Caesar Octavianus
3: Navarcha of the Antonian fleet
4: Miles classiarius of the Octavian fleet
5: Miles classiarius of the Antonian fleet

A

B

THE CIVILIS REVOLT, GERMANIA, 69–70 AD
1: L. Lucretius Celeris, *miles of Legio I Adiutrix*
2: *Optio, Legio I Adiutrix*
3: Batavian rebel auxiliary
4: Gallo-Roman *nauta*

SHORE DUTY, LATE 1ST/EARLY 2ND C AD
1: Optio Montanus Capito, *liburna* 'Aurata'; second half of 1st C
2: L. Bennius Beuza, *miles gregarius liticen*, 100 AD
3: *Faber navalis*, Misenum Fleet, 79 AD
4 & 5: *Milites*, Ravenna Fleet, 103 AD

C

THE DANUBE FLEET, ANTONINE PERIOD

1: *Tribunus* of a *Legio Adiutrix*
2: Q. Statius Rufinus
3: *Centurio* Herennius

D

THE YEARS OF ANARCHY, 3rd CENTURY AD
1: *Centurio* Aemilius Severus, trireme 'Hercules', Ravenna Fleet; late 2nd/ early 3rd C
2: T. Flavius Sabestianus, *miles*, *Centuria Philippiana*, trireme 'Victoria', Misenum Fleet; 244–249 AD
3: M. Aurelius Mausaeus Carausius; Britain, 286–293 AD

GENIO
PRAETORI
SACRVMPI
TVANIVSSE
CVNDVSPRÆ
FECTVS(oHIIII
GALLOR

E

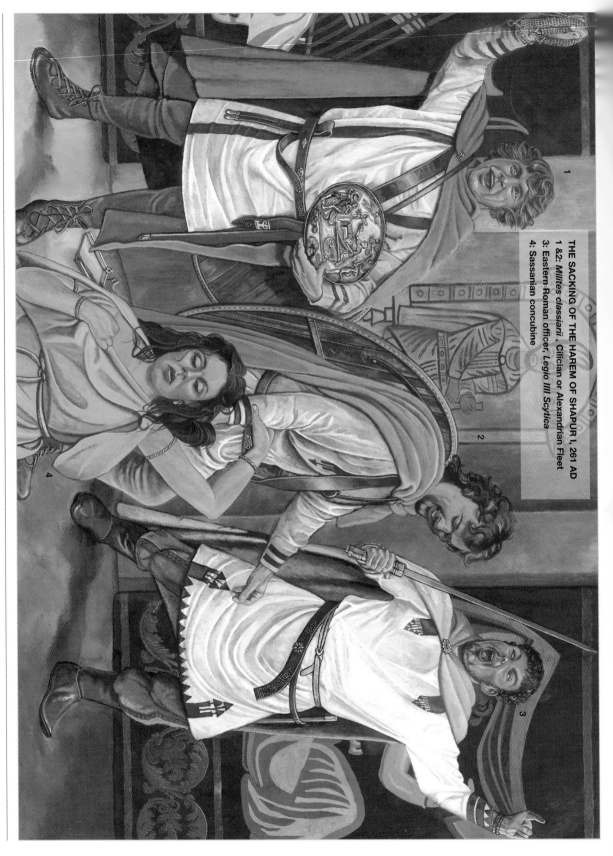

THE SACKING OF THE HAREM OF SHAPUR I, 261 AD
1 &2: *Milites classiarii*, Cilician or Alexandrian Fleet
3: Eastern Roman officer, *Legio IIII Scytica*
4: Sassanian concubine

F

NAVAL OPERATIONS ON THE RHINE, 357 AD
1: Alaman warrior
2: Roman officer, Rhine Fleet
3: Romano–Germanic naval scout
4: Roman *classiarius*, Rhine Fleet

G

DOUGGA MOSAIC

H

Armour and shields

Helmets and caps of the British Fleet marines are well illustrated in the famous 4th-century mosaic from Low Ham Villa in Somerset representing scenes from the Aeneid; a metal helmet of Intercisa style, with red crest, and a red Phrygian cap are visible behind the sides of a warship. A very interesting detail from the late 5th-century *Vergilius Romanus* codex shows the continuity of the equipment described by Vegetius for Imperial sailors and marines; it represents historic 'Trojan' warriors as late Roman fighting sailors, wearing Phrygian caps of different colours. Middle Empire pictorial sources show a general tendency to equip the marines in a lighter way than land-based troops. A thick tunic, with a heavy but short *sagum* and trousers, seems to be the usual dress of the *miles classiarius* of the 3rd century; this is well represented on the stela of T. Flavius Sabestianus from Rodosto (Bulgaria). Vegetius, however, recommended that marines should be equipped with a complete armour (*cataphracti*), or at very least half-armour (*loricati*), with helmets (*galeati*) and greaves (*ocreis muniti*).

In North African and British mosaics of the 3rd and 4th centuries men on board warships are protected by round polished shields. Vegetius recommends large, heavy shields against thrown stones, and wide shields against the use of *falces* and hooks mounted on poles (*harpagones* – Ep., V, 14). Surviving fragments of the Column of Arcadius show the naval battle fought on the Bosphorus against the Goths in 400 AD, with heavy Imperial infantrymen protected by the typical late Roman oval shields. The naval fighters from the *Vergilius Romanus* manuscript have oval shields and spears; shield surfaces are painted in green, orange, red and yellow, with bosses of Liebenau type.

Weapons

Milites classiarii of the 2nd–3rd centuries carried short swords and daggers, as attested in the funerary reliefs; swords are usually worn on the right side of the body at least until the 3rd century. While the dagger follows the traditional Imperial form the sword seems to anticipate the *semi-spatha* of the later Empire. This is visible on, e.g., the tombstone of Severus from Philippopolis; the scabbard terminates in a stylised image of interlaced facing typical of those of the early 3rd century. *Baltea* and *cingula* (belts symbolic of military service and of practical use) are clearly visible on such monuments.

The use of the javelin and spear by naval troops is well attested from tombstones of the 2nd–3rd centuries, and mosaics of the same period from Mauretania also show the use of javelins and war-axes by sailors. Throwing-spears are widely mentioned by Vegetius, as well as stones, arrows, other missiles and even *plumbatae* (lead-weighted darts). Archers and missile-throwers operated from the usual wooden towers; the fragments and drawings of the now-lost Arcadius Column show two ships full of armed men, and archers are visible in the battle scenes.

Bronze fragments of a musical instrument, possibly relating to the *gregalis* L. Bennius Beuza, from Voghenza, 100 AD. (Author's photo, courtesy Archaeological Museum, Ferrara)

33

**Naval mallet from the Comacchio ship, last quarter of 1st century BC. This ship find yielded four distinct types of mallet:
(1) parallelepiped head, in which the handle is inserted and reinforced by two wedges protruding from the hole extremities;
(2) prismatic head;
(3) horizontal head;
(4) cylindrical head, made from a single piece of wood. They have the typical shape of caulking mallets, or those used in the ancient world for repairs to the structure with nails and pegs. In all the considered specimens the axis of the handle is offset from that of the head, probably for a more effective employment of the tool. Some of them had notches on the handle, perhaps owners' marks. (From original excavation drawings; Archaeological Museum, Ferrara, courtesy Dr Fede Berti)**

Vegetius mentions the use of a particular kind of axe, the *bipennis* or double-headed axe with a very wide and sharp iron blade, used to cut the ropes of the enemy's ships (*Ep.*, IV, 46). This was a favourite weapon of the marines in close quarter-fighting, together with the sword (*Ep.* V, 15). The *falx* was probably widely used by late Imperial marines, at least in the *Classis Britannica*, as shown by a coin of Carausius. Vegetius expressly mentions it among their weapons, saying that its sharp, curved blade was useful in sea battles for cutting the opponents' rigging when attached to a pole. It survived into the Roman naval armament of the Middle Ages under the name of *drepanion*.

MISCELLANEOUS EQUIPMENT

The use of trumpets (*tubae*) for passing orders at sea is attested from both iconographic and literary sources (Dio Cassius, L, 31, 4). A sculpture from Nola, Italy, celebrating the naval victory at Actium shows *tubicines* behind Octavian who is praying to Apollo Aziacum. In the above-mentioned relief from Madrid a *tubicen* is protected by what seems to be a leather *lorica segmentata*. Recent excavations in northern Italy have recovered large fragments of a bronze musical instrument probably belonging to a *classiarius* of Dalmatian origin.

Specific naval standards (*signa*) are recorded by the sources (Prop., IV,24). Suetonius also writes that the *classiarii* had their own *aquila* and *signa*. The colour of the *vexillum* (*semeion*) of the admiral's flagship was dark blue, as was that given to Agrippa by Octavian after a naval victory (Cassius Dio, LI, 9,3). Suetonius (*Div. Aug.* XXV) states that Octavian presented a *caeruleum vexillum* (sky-blue flag) to Agrippa after his victory at Actium.

Statius Rufinus, whose mid-2nd century AD tombstone was found in Athens, served as a *classiarius* of the Misenum Fleet. His stele represents him holding either with a box of wax tablets (*codex ansatus*), or, by a different interpretation, a lamp (*lanterna*), an important means of signalling on ships. Ship's lamps like those represented on Trajan's Column have been found on the Comacchio shipwreck in Italy.

Other necessary items on warships included buckets of water (essential for putting out fires), hooks and harpoons, and wooden bailers. A short-handled, long-headed wooden mallet (Plaut., *Men.*, 2,3,52; lat. *malleus, marcus, marcellus, marculus, marceolus, martiolus*) was used for maintenance, e.g. for the preparation of new cordage, and – with an awl – for cleaning barnacles off the hull. Axes were used for maintenance, and one is clearly visible as an instrument of naval carpentery in the famous stele of the *faber navalis* P. Longidienus from Classe. The plane (*runcina*) was used to smooth wood; the late 1st-century BC Comacchio ship yielded a bailer, a plane, an axe, and nine mallets.

THE SHIPS

Construction

Ancient Mediterranean shipwrights used the 'carvel' or 'shell first' method of construction for their long, narrow warships (*navis longa*, Vitruvius, X, 14, 6). From the keel (*carinae*, Cassius Dio XLVIII, 38), with its attached stem- and stern-posts, they built the planking upwards, inserting transverse ribs of varying sizes as they progressed, their curved axis forming the cross-sectional shape of the hull. Unlike the hulls of the 'clinker-built' ships of northern Europe, the planks did not overlap each other from top to bottom; the skin (*alveus*) was formed of planks (*trabes*) held together edge to edge by a system of mortise-and-tenon joints. To reinforce the whole structure *cinctae* (*zostheres*) – girdles – were arranged to strengthen the ship's sides, also providing resistance against missiles and ramming. An inner keel or keelson incorporated the footing or step (*modius, mesodme*) for the main mast, which passed up through the deck planking, and transverse support beams reinforced the upper part of the hull. One of the excavated Nemi ships – pleasurecraft of the Emperor Caligula, which imitated warships – shows that the hull planking was sometimes covered with lead sheet attached by small copper nails; such sheathing protected the underwater parts of the hull from the accretion of barnacles and damage by marine lifeforms.

In the Mediterranean the wood most commonly used for the planking was from coniferous trees, while hardwoods such as oak and beech were employed for the keel and frames; to reduce weight the *cinctae* were made from lighter timbers such as plane-tree or larch. Pitch and vegetable glue were used from ancient times to caulk (waterproof) ships' hulls, as shown by an amphora filled with pitch found in one of the ships now preserved in the Fiumicino Museum. Vegetius gives us the materials employed for the building of *liburnae* (see below): cypress, larch, fir or pine wood, and copper nails instead of iron to avoid corrosion (V,4).

Propulsion

On the mast the main squared sail of the ship was rigged from a main yard; the Comacchio ship had cordage woven from esparto grass. A second triangular sail was often attached to the main mast, where standards were displayed. At the prow a slanting foremast or bowsprit was often rigged with a squared sail (*artemon*) designed to support the helm (*gubernaculum*, Suet., *Div. Aug.*, XVII) in controlling the manoeuvring of the ship. The helm consisted of two steering-oars protruding through slots on the opposite sides of the stern; a single helmsman usually controlled them both, if necessary – because of their weight and dimensions – by means of an extra transverse tiller (*iugum*).

Satchel-like leather bags from the Comacchio ship, last quarter of 1st century BC; a number of leather sacks (*marsupia*) of various sizes were also recovered. (From original excavation drawings; Archaeological Museum, Ferrara, courtesy Dr Fede Berti)

The main propulsion of the ship was provided by the oars. Based upon the dimensions of the rowlocks, the diameter of the oar shaft was not less than 10cm (3.9in), and during the early Empire – based on the Praeneste relief – their average length was about 4.5m (14.75ft), although the length varied in relation to the waterline. The number of oars varied with the ship's hull length, and the oarsmen were seated in levels arranged one above the other. The oars of the lower level (if present) protruded through holes in the planking furnished with leather 'boots' or collars around the oar to keep water out. Those of the upper level of rowers were

Roman trireme depicted on a marble fragment from Pozzuoli, 1st century AD, possibly representing the flagship of the admiral of the Misenum Fleet. Rome owed the design of her warships to the steady evolution of Greek and other Mediterranean patterns over many centuries; both the beaked ramming prow *(rostrum)* and the decorative upswept extension from the stern timbers *(aplustre)* are found in vase paintings as early as the 8th century BC. Note here the circular ornament attached to the *aplustre*; the decorated side-panels high at the bow and stern; the *acrostolium* protruding above the *rostrum* beak, and the turret-like superstructure on the forecastle.
RIGHT **Another panel shows a standard *(signa* or *vexilla)* mounted above the *aplustre*. (Casts, Museo della Civiltà Romana, Rome)**

fixed to rowlocks in a protruding outrigger gallery at the upper edge of the hull – this outrigger guaranteed maximum rowing efficiency and, together with the cross-sectional curvature of the hull, meant that rowers were not seated directly below one another but 'staggered' outwards from bottom to top levels. To protect the oarsmen in the top level the outrigger gallery was covered by box housings (*catafractae*), and often these were further protected by rows of the oarsmens' shields.

The sails were employed in favourable wind conditions, but were always hauled down before joining battle. Before the battle of Actium, Antony's orders to raise the sails confused the crews, since this could only have the purpose of avoiding action, which may in fact have been Antony's intention. The sails, usually of linen but also of cotton, were reinforced by leather strips and furnished with reinforced holes for the running ropes that allowed the aspect of the sail to be adjusted to suit wind conditions. The triangular 'Latin' sail, rigged slantwise and slightly advanced towards the bow, was later destined to replace the squared sail, and was the main sail of the Roman *dhromona* of the Middle Ages as well as of the Mediterranean *galerae*.

(When necessity arose, ships could be moved a certain distance from one body of water to another overland, by manpower or animal teams. Before the battle of Actium triremes of Antony's fleet were transported from the outer sea to the Gulf of Patras by way of the fortifications, along a track of newly flayed hides smeared with olive oil.)

Ship types

Warships were classified as *biremi*, *triremi*, *quadriremi* and *quinquiremi*. These categories were once assumed to refer to between two and five horizontal 'banks' or levels of oars, but the relationship between the number of levels of oars and their disposition is difficult to determine today, especially since even higher numbers than five are mentioned. For the battle of Actium, we are told that Antony constructed 'only a few triremes, but instead some ships with four and some with ten banks of oars, and all the remainder in between these two'. Today, however, it is generally accepted that three parallel, superimposed levels of rowers was the maximum number possible for practical ship-handling, and ten separate levels of oars is clearly a physical impossibility. Judging from Greek sources and practical experiments in recent years, it is now believed that the references to quadriremes and quinqueremes must refer to ships with three levels of oars, but with multiple rowers pulling some of those oars. Trireme and quinquereme were of about the same hull size, i.e. approximately 40m long and 5m wide (*c*.130ft by 16ft).

It has been suggested that the 'fours, fives, sixes', etc, may refer to the total number of men pulling the three oars in a single vertical 'stack' on the three levels. In the bireme the bottom level of rowers were seated low down, the top level at bulwark-height above them and in the intervals between those of the bottom level. In the trireme, each oarsman in the central level was seated slightly forward of the rower above him and slightly to the rear of the rower below him, each man's head roughly level with the seat of the man above. The 4th-century BC Athenian naval inventories from Peiraieus tell us that the trireme had 170 oarsmen, thus 85 per side. Of the 85, 31 rowed in the upper level, and 27 in both the middle and bottom levels. The quinquereme had 270 oarsmen, thus 135 per side, of which 23 rowed in the bottom level. The remaining 112 could thus have manned 28 two-man oars in both the top and central levels, and a single vertical 'stack' of three oars would total five rowers.

Part of a monument related to a naval battle, Ostia, 1st century AD. The small circles carved in threes at the tops of the oars almost certainly indicate a trireme. (Photo courtesy Dr Stefano Izzo)

Throughout the Imperial period the most typical warship was the *liburna*, which followed the model of the Illyrian pirates' *lémboi* and the vessels of Late Hellenistic fleets. These ships were of small dimensions, nimble and highly manoeuvrable, being the prototypes for the later *dhromona*. In particular, *liburnae* became the typical ships of all the provincial fleets, though with a trireme as flagship. One of the Lake Nemi ships was actually as much as 73m long and 24m wide (*c*.239ft x 79ft), but that found in the old harbour of Pisa, substantially intact, was only 12m (39ft) in length. It still retains its keel, keelson, mast footing, frames, and the edge of the bulwark, and it is externally reinforced by two squared and parallel *cinctae*. The holes for oars are still visible, with a well-built rowlock and traces of the leather sheaths that were fixed to the bulwark with small bronze nails to form a sort of padding between the oar and the rowlock and to prevent water entering the hull. Five rowing benches are still preserved, one of which has an incised inscription. However, the most spectacular part of this small *liburna* is the perfectly preserved *rostrum* or beak at the bow; made from a oaktree, it is covered with sheet iron, and inside this are nailed the forward ends of the hull planks.

To counter the threat of Saxon incursions in Britain either Carausius or Allectus, the usurpers of Britannia, created a new kind of ship. Known as *lusoriae*, these were small and fast, with an armed crew manning a single

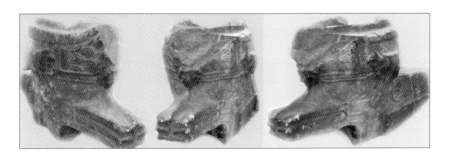

Three angles on a ship's prow with *rostrum*, a fragment of a lost monument of the Augustan period from Aquileia. The prow of this *liburna* is decorated with griffins and scales. (Museo della Civiltà Romana, Rome)

bank of oars; they were probably the high-water mark of the development of naval technology in antiquity. Representations are visible on the usurpers' coins, as well on the medallion of Constantius Chlorus celebrating his recapture of London, and on the coins of Constantine I commemorating his victory over the fleet of Licinius in 323 AD.

Scout ships were used from the late Consular period (Cassius Dio, L, 9). Four small warships of this type from the Rhine Fleet, today in the Museum fur Antike Schiffart at Mainz, give us a good idea of the shape of the *lusoriae* and of the river warships used for patrolling and police duties in the 4th century AD. One of these vessels was like a small undecked warship less than 20m (*c*.65ft) long, with one row of oars for about 20 men; it was provided with a mast-step and a towing-stake. A narrow hold area in the centre of one of these hulls shows that it could be use for transporting goods, or this may even be to accommodate the base of a dais for the use of important dignitaries. Another specimen from this group was a much larger ship designed to transport troops.

Armament and decoration

Each ship was furnished with a beak (*rostrum*), originally an extension of the keel (according to Pliny the Elder, it was used first by the Etruscans). This was a bow ram, very occasionally of wood linked laterally to the stem-post but mainly of bronze or iron (Vitruvius, X, 14, 6), with one or more prominent points (usually three). The average protruding length was 1.70–1.72m (*c*.5.5ft), and it was positioned centrally at and immediately below the waterline. A bronze three-pointed original has been found in Israel, near Athlit; this is 2m (6.5ft) long and weighs 600kg (1,320 pounds). In addition to the *rostrum* some ships were furnished with a *proembolium*, a long, strong beam used as a ramming weapon against the oarbanks of enemy ships.

Turrets (*pyrgoi*), to protect men and artillery, were erected before battle on the stern and forecastle, and might mount catapults – *onagri* and *scorpiones*. The warships would approach their adversaries from several directions at once, using artillery to hurl from a distance incendiary pots of charcoal and pitch, shooting blazing missiles and finally hurling fire-javelins. Archers and slingers were allocated to the towers, which could be dismantled if the ship needed to sail out of battle quickly (Cassius Dio, L, XXXIII, 4). Of the ships that Octavian had built for his naval wars against Sextus Pompeius, Dio (XLIX, 1,2) writes that:

His chief ground of confidence lay in the height of his vessels and the thickness of their timbers; they had been built unusually stout and unusually high, in order not only to carry the largest possible number of marines (in fact they had towers on them, in order that the men might fight from higher ground, as if from a wall), but also to withstand the attacks of the opposing vessels and at the same time bend back their beaks, since the violence of their collision would be increased thereby.

Details from the Arch of Orange showing the beaks, stern ornaments and other trophies from captured ships of Antony and Cleopatra's fleet taken to the harbour of Forum Iulii in Narbonensis (southern France). Such parts of captured ships, together with weapons and armour taken from their crews, were used to erect triumphal displays – *spoliae navales* – to celebrate naval victories such as those of Agrippa and the Gens Julia in the Actium campaign. Similar trophies adorn monuments to the gods Mars and Neptune erected by Octavian in Nicopolis, Egypt, to mark his defeat of Antony and Cleopatra (Suet., *Div. Aug.*, XVIII). (Photos author's collection)

Grave stele of the carpenter P. Longidienus, Augustan period, from Classe. (Right) detail of the image of this *faber navalis* working on the construction of a small warship; he was probably employed nearby in the yards of the Ravenna Fleet. The presence of a fleet base played a major part in local economic and demographic development; the Ravenna Fleet needed copious provisions for its 10,000 men, and materials including timber and pitch for the ships, linen for the sails, hemp for the ropes, wool and leather for the clothes and equipment of the men. By the end of the 1st century AD the area of the Po river delta on the Adriatic had attracted large numbers of craftsmen, retailers, merchants, and transporters of goods along rivers and roads. (Museo Archeologico, Ravenna)

Heavy artillery was also to be found on the fighting deck, able to shoot missiles at the enemy rowing area. Boarding-harpoons with cables could be projected by *balistae* to couple with the enemy ship; a special type of harpoon, the *harpax*, was devised by Agrippa and was fundamental to the naval victories of Octavian. The *sideroi cheiroi* ('iron hands') were grappling irons able to grasp individual sailors or parts of their ships. Cassius Dio describes a naval action in which:

> The followers of Sextus Pompeius alarmed their opponents by the way they dashed across the waves, and they also damaged some ships by assailing them with a rush and ripping open the parts that were beyond the banks of oars; but since [Sextus' ships] were assailed with missiles from the towers at the moment of attack and were brought alongside by grappling irons, they suffered no less harm than they inflicted. And Caesar's forces, when they came into close conflict and boarded the enemy ships, proved superior.

The 'dolphins' that are mentioned in some sources were incendiary pots, suspended and sometimes dropped from a beam raised over the *rostrum;* these were successfully used by Octavian's fleet at Actium.

Beam-heads were often strengthened and decorated with bronze animal heads (*protoma*), and the balustrades by double-faced *Hermae*, as in the specimen from Nemi. Sometimes a divinity *protoma* or a statue like a later figurehead (*polena*) was placed under or corresponding with the *acrostolium*, the main ornamental protuberance at the prow. From the 1st century BC warships were distinguished by a particular circular emblem placed on the *aplustre*, the fishtail-shaped ornamental structure rising from the stern. To ward off bad luck, large eyes were painted on the prow. After a naval victory the prow of the ship was decorated with flower-garlands (Dio Cassius, LI,5,4); after a defeat and capture its beak might be hacked off for incorporation in the victor's triumphal monument, as hunters display the heads of their kills.

The world of the marines, like that of all Roman soldiers, was full of religion and superstition: on the stern of the ship an altar was often placed in honour of the protective divinity of the ship, from which it took its name. This name was normally indicated on the side or on a *stylís*, a kind of tablet fixed to the sternpost. The goddess Isis was one the most popular among sailors, together with Bacchus, Apollo, Minerva, the Dioscuri and, of course, Poseidon (Neptune). Women or other persons

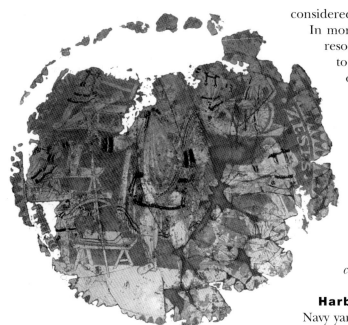

considered impure were not allowed on board ship. In moments of the greatest danger and as a last resort the whole ship's company would pray to the sacred anchor, the largest of those on board. During the Empire anchors (*agkurai*) were of iron, harpoon-shaped, but sometimes covered with wood – e.g. the specimen from Lake Nemi.

A picture of a late-Roman *liburna* in the *Notitia Dignitatum* manuscript in the Bodleian Library, Oxford, represents the decoration and armament of a 5th-century warship used in the desperate wars against barbarian raiders. It shows a bronze *rostrum* in multicoloured steps surmounted by the Christian symbol, and *catafractae* along the sides.

Harbours and naval yards

Navy yards where warships were based or repaired were called *navalia*. Originally two were located in Rome itself: the *navalia superiora* (near the Campus Martius), and *inferiora* (near the mouth of the Cloaca Maxima, and linked with the commercial quarter called the Emporium). However, by the 1st century AD they were already little more than museums (and Procopius, writing in the 6th century, even says that the warship believed to have been used by the legendary hero Aeneas was kept in one of them).

Important military harbours in Italy included the Portus Iulius, near Cuma, created by Agrippa in 37 BC. The Portus Misenatis, base of the Misenum Fleet, was from 31 BC the most important naval base in the western Mediterranean. It was large enough to accommodate the admiral's flagship, described as a *hexeres* (six banks of oars), *triremi*, *quadriremi* (Pliny the Younger, Ep. VI, 16, 8), *quinquiremi* and *liburnae*. The Portus Ravennatis, housing the Ravenna fleet, could accomodate up to 250 ships. To help the construction of the harbour a canal was built to link it to the River Po; due to progressive silting of the harbour, from the 2nd century AD a new military harbour was built at Classe a few miles away, partially over the Castra Classis Praetoriae Ravennatis or fleet camp.

WAR AT SEA

The main Roman method of naval fighting, from the Punic Wars onwards, was to transfer their superior land tactics to the naval environment by drawing alongside enemy ships and boarding them. To this end they fitted gangplanks called *corvi* (ravens) at the ships' extremities, the *corvus* being attached to a raised, pivoting post about 8m (26ft) high at the ship's bow and/or stern. This boarding bridge, about 1.20m (*c.*4ft) wide, was constructed in two sections, with parapets on either side. The end was swivelled out and dropped by means of a rope and pulley, driving a spike under the end into the enemy ship's deck; two files of soldiers could then cross over, protected by their own shields and the parapets. Some modern

A gilded glass cover of Tetrarchic or Constantinian date, early 4th century AD. It shows an officer of a naval dockyard (*fabrica navalis*), wearing a fringed *lacerna* cloak and carrying a staff of command. All the tunics of the men in the background are confined by military belts fastened with old-fashioned buckles of 3rd-century type. (Musei Vaticani, Rome)

historians argue that the *corvus* must have made Roman ships unstable, and cite as evidence the heavy losses incurred by Roman ships to storms during the Punic Wars. However, Vitruvius writing in the Augustan period still included the *corvus* among the *marinae machinae* used for boarding (X, 13, 8).

Before battle, it was usual to order the rowers to let their oars rest in the water. When the attack began the fleets usually tried to advance with both their wings forward in a crescent formation, hoping to envelop the enemy or otherwise to break their formation. The typical naval tactic of ramming and the use of artillery to set fire to enemy ships is well exemplified in the battle of Actium. We are told that Antony had built on his ships 'lofty towers, and he had put aboard a large number of men, who could thus fight from walls'. Antony's heavy ships stood like a wooden wall on the sea, but made an easy target for the artillery shooting from a distance; they were then ripped open by the beaks of Octavian's more manoeuvrable *liburnae*, and set ablaze by incendiary missiles launched from the *machinae* placed on the latters' decks. Although smaller and swifter, Octavian's ships were still armoured on all sides; even if they did not sink a vessel at the first ramming attack they could back their oars and withdraw, before either ramming the same vessel again or attacking another ship,

> …and then against still others, in order that their assault upon any vessel might be so far as possible unexpected. For since they dreaded the long-range missiles of the enemy no less than their fighting at close quarters, they wasted no time either in the approach or in the encounter, but running up suddenly so as to reach their target before the enemy's archers could do their work, they would inflict damage or else cause just enough disturbance to escape being held, and then would retire out of range.

Two or three ships might fall upon the same enemy vessel at once, some doing all the damage they could while the others drew the attention of the enemy's weapons crews. In Octavian's fleet the ship-handling sailors and the rowers endured the most hardship and fatigue, while on Antony's side it was the marines who bore the brunt of the fighting:

> Consequently each gained advantages over the other; the one party would run in upon the lines of oars projecting from the ships and shatter the blades, and the other party, fighting from the higher level, would sink them with stones and engines. On the other hand, there were also disadvantages on each side: the one party might do no damage to the enemy when it approached, and the other party, if it failed to sink a vessel which it rammed, might be hemmed in and fighting an unequal contest.

Warships and crews, from the *Vergilius Romanus* codex, late 5th century AD. The earliest representation of the light waships termed *dhromones* is shown in this manuscript, produced either in Italy or in Britain in about 500 AD. The marines wear thick felt Phrygian caps (*kamelaukia*), heavy cloaks and tunics; the different colours of the shields may represent the different *contubernia* or squads. Similar troops to these participated in a disastrous expedition against the Vandals in 468 AD. (Ms Lat 3867, Biblioteca Apostolica, Città del Vaticano)

We can imagine from this description how terrible a naval battle in ancient times could be. Warships, some of them already blazing, smashed against each other with a horrific noise of broken wood amid the shouts, trumpet-blasts and screams of men fighting upon the decks. The sea was littered with wreckage and broken human bodies; sailors who tried to swim for it were hit with oars, while marines wearing heavy armour faced death by drowning. The savagery of such a fight is well described by Dio:

> ...Caesar's men damaged the lower parts of the ships all around, crushed the oars, snapped off the rudders, and, climbing on the decks, seized hold of some of the foe and pulled them down, pushed off others, and fought with yet others, since they were now equal to them in numbers... Some, and particularly the sailors, perished by the smoke before the flame so much as approached them, while others were roasted in the midst of it as though in ovens. Others were consumed in their armour when it became heated. There were still others, who, before they should suffer such a death, or when they were half-burned, threw off their armour and were wounded by shots from a distance, or again leaped into the sea and were drowned, or were struck by their opponents and sank, or were mangled by sea-monsters [sic]. The only ones to find a tolerable death, considering the sufferings which prevailed, were those killed by their fellows in return for the same service, or else who killed themselves, before any such fate could befall them. These had no tortures to endure, and when they were dead they had the burning ships for their funeral pyres.

When a ship caught fire under any circumstances the men first used first the drinking-water butts to try to extinguish the flames, and if this failed they tried to use seawater, but this was not practical in the chaos of a battle (it was even claimed that salt water actually made the flames burn more vigorously). Then, as Cassius Dio wrote, 'when they found themselves getting the worst of it in this respect also, they heaped on the blaze their thick mantles and the corpses... but later... when the wind raged furiously, the flames flared up more than ever, fed by this very fuel'.

SELECT BIBLIOGRAPHY

Béjaoui, F., S. Mansour, et al, *Mosaici Romani di Tunisia* (Paris, 1994)

Blas de Roblès, J.M., & C. Sintes, *Sites et Monuments Antiques de l'Algérie* (Aix en Provence, 2003)

Chiarucci , P., *Settimio Severo e la Legione Seconda Partica* (Albano Laziale, 2006)

Coussin, P, *Les Armes Romaines* (Paris, 1926)

Cowan, R., *Roman Legionary 58 BC–AD 69*, (Warrior 71) (Oxford, 2003)

Daremberg-Saglio, *Dictionnaire des Antiquités Grecques et Romaines* (Paris, 1877–1919)

Fede Berti, *Fortuna Maris, la nave romana di Comacchio* (Bologna, 1990)

Forestier, A., *The Roman Soldier* (London, 1928)

Franzoni, C., *Habitus atque habitude militis, monumenti funerari di militari nella Cisalpina Romana* (Rome, 1987)

Gore, R., 'The dead do tell tales at Vesuvius' in *National Geographic*, Vol.165 (May 1984) 557 ff

Guzzo, G.P., *Storie da un 'eruzione: Pompei, Ercolano, Oplontis* (Milan, 2003)

Henniquiau, M. & J. Martin, *La Marine Antique, 2* (Pantin, 1999)

Le Bohec, Y., *L'armée Romaine* (Paris, 1989)

Liberati, A.M., 'Navigare con gli antichi', in *Archeo 8* (1997) 45–93

Liberati, A.M., E. Silverio & F.Silverio, 'L'esercito e la marina militare nell'antica Roma', in *Roma Archaeologica 18–19* (July 2003)

MacDowall, S., *Late Roman Infantryman 236–565 AD*, Warrior 9 (London, 1994)

Mason, D.J.P., *Roman Britain and the Roman Navy* (Port Stroud, 2003)

Mendel, G., *Catalogue des sculptures grecques, romaines et byzantines*, 3 vols (Rome, 1966)

Parker, A.J., *Ancient Shipwrecks of the Medierranean and the Roman Provinces*, BAR International Series 580 (Oxford, 1992)

Santa Maria Scrinari, V., *Sculture Romane di Aquileia* (Rome, 1972)

Saxtorph, N.M., *Warriors and Weapons 3000 BC–AD 1700* (London, 1972)

Sekunda, N., *Republican Roman Army 200–104 BC*, (Men-at-Arms 291) (London, 1996)

Sumner, G., *Roman Military Clothing (1) 100 BC–AD 200*, (MAA 374) (Oxford, 2002)

Sumner, G., *Roman Military Clothing (2) AD 200-400*, (MAA 390) (Oxford, 2003)

various, in *Genti nel Delta, Uomini, territori e culto dall'antichità all'Alto Medieovo* (Ferrara, 2007)

various, in *Le tre vite del Papiro di Artemidoro, voci e squardi dall'Egitto Greco-Romano* (Milan, 2006)

Walker, S. & P. Higgs, *Cleopatra regina d'Egitto* (Milan, 2000)

**Principal ancient sources
(see Loeb Classical Library translations):**

Ammianus Marcellinus, *Res Gestae*; Appian, *Civil Wars, Roman History*; Cassius Dio, *Roman History*; Cicero, *Philippicae*; Constantine Porphyrogenitus, *De Ceremoniis Aulae Byzantinae*; Florus, *Epitome of Roman History*; Herodian, *History of the Empire from the Time of Marcus Aurelius*; Horatius, *Odes, Epodes*; Justinian, *Digest* or *Pandects*; Livy, *History of Rome from the Founding of the City*; Plautus, *Poenulus, Menaechmi, Miles Gloriosus*; Pliny the Elder, *Historia Naturalis*; Pliny the Younger, *Epistulae*; Plutarch, *Parallel Lives (Antonius)*; Propertius, *Elegies*; Pseudo-Hyginus, *The Fortifications of the Camp*; Scriptores Historia Augusta (SHA); Synkellos, *The Chronography*; Suetonius, *The Twelve Caesars*; Tacitus, *Annals, Histories*; Ulpian, *Institutiones in Digestum*; Vegetius, *The Military Art*; Vitruvius, *De Architectura*; Zonaras, *Extracts from History*.

PLATE COMMENTARIES

A: BATTLE OF ACTIUM, 31 BC

A1: M. Vipsanius Agrippa
Reconstruction based upon his portraits and statues, and the Praeneste mosaic. Following Virgil's description, he wears a *corona rostrata*, the decoration for a victorious admiral. His muscled armour, worn over a leather *subarmale* arming doublet, is copied from the exceptional specimen from Cueva del Jarro, Spain. His *tunica* of pale blue is decorated with the purple *clavi* typical of his senatorial rank; at the time of Augustus the *laticlavius* was reduced to two parallel *clavi* of red-purple. In the right hand he holds a *hasta navalis*; the sword illustrated is copied from the specimen from Comacchio. Plausible footwear would be soft white leather *cothurni* or *calcei mullei* of Greek type.

A2: C.G. Caesar Octavianus
The future Emperor Augustus, also reconstructed from the Praeneste mosaic and from the statue of Cirta, holds an Attic helmet with the 'shining cheekguards' mentioned by Virgil decorated with embossed thunderbolts and, on the skull, the *Sidus Julium*, symbol of the Gens Julia. The colour of his armour – obviously painted, with appliqués realized in gilded brass or even gold – is from the Palestrina mosaic. The two elements of the *lorica* are fastened on both sides, by a system identical to that of the Prima Porta armour. Under it he wears a leather *subarmale* with linen *pteryges*. His dyed wool tunic is decorated with purple *laticlavi* and gold thread damask, while his scarlet *paludamentum* is pinned to the leather armour with a gold *fibula*. He has a small *parazonium* with an eagle-head hilt worn at his right side, copied from the Arch of Orange, and his *gladius* is a Pompei specimen. The sources describe Octavian with the *hasta summa imperii* (spear of supreme command) during the battle of Actium. Note his elaborate yellow *cothurni* footwear.

A3: Navarcha of the Antonian fleet
This defeated senior officer is copied from the famous monument of Praeneste, representing a warship of Antony's fleet surrendering to Octavian. He wears a *thorax pholidotos* (scale armour) of Hellenistic style, with *humeralia* (shoulder pieces) fastened with laces on the breast. The metal scales are fixed to a leather jupon to which are sewn rows of linen *pteryges*; and note the military *zonì* (sash) around the breast, and the off-white *angusticlavia* tunic with the usual couple of *clavi*. The *hasta navalis* is a specimen from Ornavasso. The greaves represented on the monument are similar to those of the Aquileia reliefs, showing trophies of naval warfare. His shield is still of the old late Consular type, reinforced with a wooden 'barleycorn' boss and with bronze guttering at top and bottom only.

A4: Miles classiarius of the Octavian fleet
This marine is also copied from the Praeneste relief. The main characteristics of his protective equipment are the pseudo-Corinthian bronze helmet with leather cheek-guards; his leather muscled cuirass with directly attached leather *pteryges*; and his large oval shield, decorated with Neptune's trident. The Musolina-style tunic is of the blue-grey (iron-blue) colour described by Plautus. Closed *calcei* in brown leather have been reconstructed after a fragment found in the Comacchio ship.

A5: Miles classiarius of the Antonian fleet
From a terracotta lamp in the British Museum. Note his felt armour (*coactile*) and the *subarmale*. This armour is probably identical to that of contemporary Egyptian bodyguards, made of felt strips and thickly padded; similar armour is also shown on gravestones from Sora (Frosinone) and Modena. His sword is from the Idria specimen, and the *caligae* – worn here over socks – are from the Comacchio ship. His shield is decorated on its upper part with Cleopatra's cartouche painted in natural colours. Note also the Egyptian bracelet on his right arm.

B: THE CIVILIS REVOLT IN GERMANIA, 69–70 AD

B1: L. Lucretius Celeris, miles of Legio I Adiutrix
Some of the figures on the Mainz Praetorium pillars represent soldiers of this legion, newly raised among the *milites classiarii* of the Misenum Fleet. His helmet of Weisenau type is decorated with the embossed dolphins visible on the sculpture. He wears two garments: an over-tunic, of muslin cloth in a blue colour, and a sleeveless leather arming doublet (*corium*), which is reconstructed after fragments from Vindonissa and also visible on Rhine tombstones. Note his sword, still of old Mainz type. The boots (*calcei*) are after the Martre de Veyre specimen, which appears identical to those visible in the Mainz sculpture; ancestors of the later *campagus*, they left the upper part of the feet visible. The device on his shield has been reconstructed following the original source, where the motifs flanking the eagle are not thunderbolts but wings.

B2: Optio, Legio I Adiutrix
From the same source, this *optio* wears a *lorica ferrata* (mail armour) over a *subarmale*. The shape of the armour is copied from finds at Vindonissa: made from alternate rows of very small punched and riveted bronze rings, each about 0.5cm (0.2in) in diameter. The linen *subarmale* is copied from Trajan's Column: a sort of tunic, furnished with small *pteryges* at the shoulders only, and with side vents to ease movement, corresponding to those of the mail armour.

Aureus (gold coin) of M. Vipsanius Agrippa, 18 BC. This commander, victorious by sea and land, is shown here wearing both the *corona rostrata* and *corona muralis* – compare with Plate A1. (Museo della Civiltà Romana, Rome)

Recently found at Ravenna during the excavations of Classe harbour, this mid- to late-1st century AD monument or *cippus* commemorates Montanus Capito, an *optio* serving on a *liburna* named 'Aurata' ('Golden') – see Plate C1. The baldric may be an insignia of some kind rather than a weapon belt

B3: Batavian rebel auxiliary

This warrior of Civilis' forces is also based mainly on the Mainz reliefs. He is outfitted with a Krefeld-Gelduba helmet, comprising a skull of Weisenau type trimmed with fur. The army of Civilis was highly Romanized, so this warrior is dressed like a Roman *auxiliarius*, though with a Germanic tunic copied from a specimen from Bernuthsfeld – despite Tacitus' claim that 'For their covering all they wear is a mantle fastened with a clasp or, for want of it, with a thorn.'. Over the tunic he wears a leather corselet, scalloped at the lower hem and the short sleeves, with a double reinforcement border in leather and small bronze bosses, as visible on Trajan's Column. He is armed with three spears, and a sword worn from a baldric and copied from a 1st-century AD specimen now in Njimegen Museum. His shield is a parallel-sided oval reconstructed from fragments found in Batavia; the blazon is hypothetically reconstructed from the stele of a Batavian in Roman service, with the colours given for the Batavi in the much later *Notitia Dignitatum*.

B4: Gallo-Roman *nauta*, 1st century AD

The main source for this reconstruction is the Paris pilaster depicting sailors. Besides his helmet of Coolus-Mannheim type this fighting seaman is armed with a spear and a trapezoidal Celtic shield with a central *spina*. He wears a *paenula* cloak but woven with a Celtic pattern, taken from a mantle fragment from Dydimoi. The Celtic trousers, in wool and linen, are typically baggy; the tunic is copied from the La Vachères warrior specimen, with long sleeves and cuffed wrists. Heavy embossed and padded leather armour, as visible on Celtic coins of King Dumnorix, consists of a coat open in front, divided in rhomboidal patterns and reinforced with bronze nails. His closed boots of Celtic pattern are copied from a fragment of a Gallo-Roman shoe, in natural leather and furnished with loops for the laced fastening.

C: SAILORS ON SHORE DUTY, LATE 1st/EARLY 2nd CENTURY AD

C1: Montanus Capito, *Optio* of the *liburna* 'Aurata'; second half of 1st century

This marine junior officer is copied from his Ravenna memorial. Under bronze muscled armour with nipples of inlaid silver he wears a padded garment furnished with thick *pteryges*. A particularity of his *hasta navalis* is the presence of two spheroids in the middle, similar to later representations of weighted *pila*; the spearhead visible on the memorial suggests a kind of command spear or perhaps a sort of *pilum navalis*. A leather baldric with gold and silver bosses impressed with the image of the Emperor Vespasian runs over his right shoulder, supporting a Pompei-type sword. Sculpted elements on the *cingulum* make clear that it was a plated belt with an attached *pugio* and two apron straps, here all reconstructed after Pompei specimens. The open *caligae*, with incorporated *perones*, are from the Comacchio finds.

C2: L. Bennius Beuza, *miles gregarius liticen*, c.100 AD

The Dalmatian marine reconstructed here, from a frieze of marine musicians at Ostia, wears a tunic similar to that worn by other Dalmatian soldiers on 1st century stelae, in the colour mentioned by Plautus (this iron-grey shade in a military context is visible on some cloth fragments from Mons Claudianus). His leather belt with simple apron straps is hidden here by a satchel of a type found with the Comacchio ship. The feet are enclosed in *socci* – shoes without laces and with the upper part closed, low on the ankle.

C3: *Faber navalis, Classis Praetoria Misenatis*, 79 AD

This marine craftsman of the Misenum Fleet is based on the famous skeletal remains found on the beach at Herculaneum, whose physical aspects were reconstructed by the archaeologists (see Gore in Bibliography); he was about 37 years old and 1.8m (5ft 10in) tall. Here he is dressed in a sleeveless leather garment based on fragments from Comacchio, with small oval or round patches sewn on to protect the weaker areas; this is worn over a *subarmale*. He wears a red-brown *lacerna* cloak fringed at the extremities. The marine has two belts, completely faced with 21 silver embossed plates, to which are attached his *pugio* and *gladius*; the apron straps terminate in hinged pendants, identical to a specimen from Tekjie. Carpentry tools found in a bag on his back included a hammer with attached adze, two chisels, and a hook.

C4 & 5: *Milites, Classis Praetoria Ravennatis*, 103 AD

Overall these marines of the Ravenna Fleet are copied from Trajan's Column. Their tunics are based on specimens from Dydimoi, showing the famous bunched neck knot typical of the period. One of them wears a leather belt with apron pendants copied from Tekije specimens, just visible at the waist. On the back, attached to the belt, a small dagger (*clunaculum*) might be worn. The pickaxes (*dolabrae*) are copied from Vindonissa specimens, as is the bronze blade-case (C5). Of interest is the hexagonal shield (C4), with appliqués in copper alloy and embossed friezes, showing a trident and four successive floral/vegetal patterns centred on the *umbo*. The naval *lanterna* is from the Comacchio finds.

D: THE DANUBE FLEET, ANTONINE PERIOD

D1: *Tribunus* of a *Legio Adiutrix*

This marine officer has a pseudo-Attic type helmet with a bronze skull decorated in gilded silver and cheekguards complete with ears. The body protection is a magnificent *subarmale* and a rigid leather *corium* corselet; the *subarmale* is formed from layers of linen, and especially decorated with fringed *pteryges* at the shoulders and waist. He wears silver *phalerae* awards. The dagger belt (*cingulum*) has squared openwork plates copied from a find from Viminacium, and *balteola* apron straps fitted with bronze nails and ending in half-moons and leaf-shaped pendants. Note the ring-pommel sword just visible behind his hexagonal *scutum*, which has appliqué decorations in copper alloy of dolphins and tridents and an embossed mask. His closed boots (*cothurni venatici*) are from Dydimoi specimens; these did not have laces.

D2: Q. Statius Rufinus

The tunic of this *classiarius* (whose name translates literally as 'Statius the small red one') has short sleeves, and considering that this man was in service in Athens he probably wears some local clothing. The colour of the tunic is that described by Plautus for the *nautae*. A fringed cloth sash knotted around the waist (*zona militaris*) was undoubtedly used to hold the short dagger. He holds a *codex ansatus* (box with handle for carrying writing tablets) in his left hand. On his feet he wears a sort of *calcei-perones* over socks (*udones*), here copied from Mons Claudianus and Vindolanda specimens.

D3: *Centurio Herennius*

On his grave stele Herennius is shown in a woollen mantle, and a very broad tunic with wide sleeves, probably a *dalmatica*. The baldric with gold bosses (*cingulum bullatum*), just visible under the mantle, is copied from that of the Fayoum Hadrianic officer from Hawara. His staff of rank is in gilded wood.

E: THE YEARS OF ANARCHY, 3rd CENTURY AD

E1: Aemilius Severus, *centurio* of the trireme 'Hercules'; *Classis Praetoria Ravennatis*, late 2nd/first quarter 3rd century

The centurion's *tunica* is a short *dalmatica* of red colour, decorated with *clavi*. It is hidden here by his *paenula* cape of semicircular or oval shape, made of heavy wool (*gausape*); bronze buttons and loops for fastening have been found in the Adriatic context, and the lower edge was knotted with a leather thong which passed through fasteners. The blue (*venetus*) cape is also decorated with *clavi*, based on the probable mariner represented in an illuminated papyrus. The nailed shoes (*calcei*) reach to the ankle and are cut from a single piece of leather; the laceholes and the back were reinforced with sheepskin lining, and an additional reinforcement strip was sewn right round the bottom part of the uppers.

E2: T. Flavius Sabestianus, *miles, Classis Praetoria Pia Vindex Misenensis*, of the *Centuria Philippiana*, in service on the trireme 'Victoria', 244–249

The marine Sabestianus wears a heavily folded or padded tunic, visible on other monuments of that century and similar to some Sarmatian heavy coats. On his stele the heavy rectangular cloak (*sagum*) shows a small tassel or knot at the lower corner (see page 19), where a bronze ring was possibly attached to allow the fastening of the cloak to the other shoulder. The monument also shows shows a simple waist belt and a *semispatha* sword at his left side. The small round shield has been reconstructed after specimens and fragments from Dura Europos, made of poplar planks glued edge to edge and finished with a leather border sewn all around; a mosaic from Cirta shows marines with a similar shield painted in dark green with a decorative border of laurel leaves. His nailed *socci* are copied from a find from Portchester Castle, England. Here the upper is composed of two pieces, and the boot is fastened by a side thong; there were at least two soles, the thinner inside, the thicker outside. The short naval javelin, in ash wood with an iron point, is painted dark green like those in the Cirta mosaic.

E3: M. Aurelius Mausaeus Carausius, 286–293

The coins of Carausius, the usurping ruler of Britannia, shed light on his military equipment, inspired by the sea-god Neptune and with distinctive symbols of imperial power. His helmet is a cavalry sports Heddernheim type. Just visible in his left hand he holds a Greek *causia* flat cap – here modelled on the specimen recovered at Vindonissa – as a further symbol of seapower. His armour is a *squama*, the scales fixed to a linen backing with linen cords and stitches as in the Carpow fragment. The leather *thoracomacus* beneath it is from the Tetrarchs monument. The greaves, copied from the 3rd-century specimen from the Rhine near Noviomagus, are of silvered bronze and embossed with a three-dimensional figure of Mars. Imperial garments comprise a large circular purple-fringed *paludamentum*, pure white (*candida*) tunic, and very close-fitted *anaxyrides*. The low *calcei* boots are in

2nd-century AD grave stele of Statius Rufinus, a *miles classiarius* of the Misenum Fleet, found in Athens – see Plate D2. (Drawing by Graham Sumner)

Romano-British style, made of soft leather, coloured in purple with stitched gold fasteners around the elaborate openwork. The splendid *signum* held by Carausius is copied from his coinage; it is decorated with bronze, copper alloy, silver and gilded glass elements, with a platform surmounted by two winged victories.

F: THE SACKING OF THE HAREM OF SHAPUR I, 261 AD

F1 &2: *Milites classiarii* of the Cilician or Alexandrian Fleet

These marines are based on the Dougga (Thugga) mosaic – see Plate H. Their woollen sleeved tunics follow Dura specimens, and show two vertical *clavi*. They are worn together with a thick woollen *sagum* cloak and Eastern-style trousers. Belts and weaponry have also been borrowed from Dura specimens. The external surface of the shield – obscured here – was covered with hide and lavishly painted.

F3: Eastern Roman officer, *Legio IIII Scytica*

Reconstructed from a imposing statue from Urfa-Edessa, this figure – perhaps a *tribunus* or *primipilus*? – is dressed in an eastern Persian style of tunic and a linen cloak, both reconstructed from fragments found in Palmyra. The tunic is decorated vertically down from the shoulder with red-purple *lanceolae*, probably rank symbols. He wears baggy Persian trousers (*sarabara*) decorated with woollen appliqué in dark purple. The original source shows the tunic fastened with a double cloth belt around the waist, closed by a unique buckle pointing towards the left side of the body – a system visible on different statues from Palmyra. The boots are copied from 3rd-century specimens from Achmim-Panopolis.

F4: Sassanian concubine

She is reconstructed after the Bishapur and Dura frescoes.

G: NAVAL OPERATIONS ON THE RHINE, 357 AD

G1: Alaman warrior

This reconstruction follows the rich graves of the Rhine border and the descriptions of the ancient authors. Ammianus describes long, thick hair dyed red with natural substances. The narrow, long-sleeved woollen tunic is decorated with trim in red-purple silk. Note his woollen close-fitting trousers, and typical Germanic boots copied from specimens found in Marx-Etzel. The shield is brightly painted, copied from the *insignia* of an Alamanic tribe, the Bucinobantes, recruited as *auxilium palatinum* into the Roman army. We illustrate a typical Germanic javelin or *angon* (*jaculum*); other weapons might include a throwing axe or *francisca* tucked into the belt, and a yew-wood Germanic bow about 2m (6ft 6in) long.

G2: Roman officer of the Rhine Fleet

He wears an iron helmet of Ausburg-Pfersee type, sheathed in gilded silver. His imposing muscled armour might have mobile shoulder-guards, and shows lappets around the lower abdomen. It is worn over a *thoracomacus* of felt lined with cotton or coarse silk, and the *pteryges* hanging from the waist are like those represented on the *Ilias Ambrosiana*, fringed with dark purple. According to Vegetius the marines and sailors of the *lusoriae* or *exploratoriae scaphae* were dressed completely in *venetus*-colour, i.e. sea-blue. His clothing, especially the *sagum* and the *bracae*, presents a mixed Romano-Germanic style, as was usual on the *limes*.

Severan period stele of C. Aemilius Severus, from Classe. This centurion, of Pannonian origin, served on the trireme 'Hercules' for 22 years. He is represented holding the *vitis* in his right hand and a scroll in the left. (Museo Arcivescovile, Ravenna; photo courtesy Dr Fede Berti)

G3: Romano-Germanic naval scout

Apart from his ridged Sassanian-style helmet, copied from the Worms specimen, his whole armament and clothing is mainly Germanic in fashion, although his military belt in *Kerbschnitt* style and the shield pattern are typical of the late Roman *limitanei* along the Rhine and Danube frontiers.

G4: Roman *classiarius* of the Rhine Fleet

This marine is reconstructed after the Lyon seal that shows the city of Mainz, but supplemented with other archaeological details. The ridge-style helmet from Augst fits well with the *classiarius* helmet visible on the Ham mosaic, furnished with a red crest. His simple mail armour is worn over a leather jerkin of the same shape; a recent interpretation of the Thorsberg find by German archaeologists suggests that silvered clasps were used for shoulder fastenings while small hooks were used for fastening the breast. The sleeved tunic is made of an undyed wool-linen mix and decorated with typical *orbiculi* and *segmenta* of the late Empire. His weapons are a *culter venatorius* and a sword, here copied from the Idesheim specimen, and a light javelin (*verutum*).

H: MOSAIC, 'ODYSSEUS AND THE SIRENS', 3rd CENTURY AD

This famous mosaic from Thugga (Dougga), now in the Bardo Museum, Tunisia, is one of the best representations of a 3rd-century warship and lightly-equipped fighting seamen. The captain is dressed in a white *exomis* and a conical *pilos* cap of white felt. The mariners may represent seamen of the *Classis Alexandrina* or *Syriaca*. They wear off-white, long-sleeved tunics, two of which show red *clavi*. Their rectangular cloaks are in light green, and are fastened with a *fibula* at the right shoulder; they are arranged so as to leave the neck of the tunic visible. The oval shields – which find a parallel in the Dura specimens – seem to have brown leather rims sewn all round, and are decorated with at least three devices.The vessel itself shows exceptional details of Roman African and Eastern warships. Note the small beak shaped like an extension of the keel; above this, a divine image, probably identified with the name of the ship; the *catafractae* covering the rowlocks; the steering oar; the cabin-like superstructure ahead of the upswept stern decoration; and the general impression of decorative painting. Note also the *aurica* foresail rigged in addition to the squared mainsail, and the spars painted in yellow and green.

INDEX